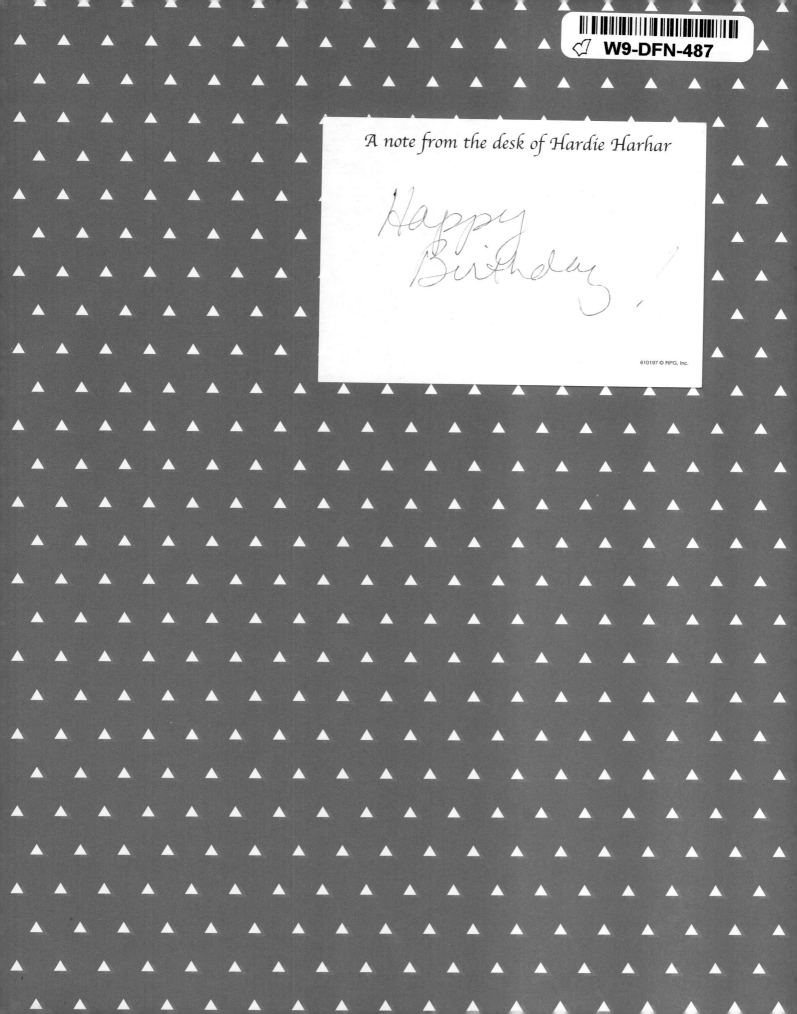

AMERICAN EXPRESS® PRESENTS
TOP CHEFS OF THE TRIANGLE

A portion of the proceeds from the sale of American Express® Presents Top Chefs of The Triangle *will be donated to The Inter-Faith Food Shuttle, which rescues thousands of pounds of prepared and perishable food each day and immediately transports it to soup kitchens and shelters feeding the Triangle's poor and homeless people. In 1995, more than 100 volunteers collected in excess of 2,000,000 pounds of food which created almost 1,500,000 meals—all at no charge—all without taxpayer funds.*

In addition, a portion of the proceeds will also be donated to Share Our Strength's Taste of the Nation. Presented by American Express and Calphalon, Taste of the Nation is the largest nationwide culinary benefit to fight hunger. An annual series of food and wine tastings are held in April in more than 100 cities across the country. Since 1988, Taste of the Nation events have raised more than $22,000,000. 100% of ticket sales are distributed to anti-hunger organizations.

▼

Dedication

This book is dedicated to the 105 men and women volunteers of The Inter-Faith Food Shuttle who give unselfishly of their time and their hearts. Each week they collect prepared and perishable food from over 200 restaurants and other donors and deliver it to the agencies and shelters that feed up to 3,600 of the Triangle's poor and homeless people each day.

About This book

American Express® Presents Top Chefs of the Triangle has been written for the home cook. Each of the 270 recipes submitted has been scaled for 6 portions, unless otherwise noted. The recipes have been tested in a home kitchen using a conventional stove and everyday cookware.

The recipes were chosen by the contributing chefs, and, for the most part, we have preserved their originally-submitted ingredients and methods. It is for this reason that you may see some variation in instructions; for example, the timing of sautéing shallots until they are translucent. We have, however, tried to standardize quantities of ingredients to conform to an actual measurement, such as 1 cup of chopped onions, instead of one medium onion, chopped.

With a few noted exceptions, all of the ingredients listed in this book can be purchased at Hannaford Food and Drug Superstores or Wellspring Grocery. Throughout the book there are "Editor's Notes" explaining alternative ingredients, or sources for the listed ingredients if they are difficult to locate.

We have provided a "Cook's Notes & Glossary" section beginning on page 143 to help clarify the description of some ingredients and methods.

TABLE OF CONTENTS

▼

FOREWORD

by Fred Benton

Memories of the Triangle restaurant scene, as durable as spiders' thread, weave a delicious design of dining experiences and the men and women who were the provenances. These places and people are part of our gustatory past and present.

During the Sixties and early Seventies the "food-scape" was culinarily sparse, relegated to barbecue huts, steak houses and coffee shops. Ethnic food opportunities were limited and sanitized to suit the American taste.

It is generally accepted that two individuals in particular began to define our contemporary restaurant scene during the latter part of this period: Theodore "Ted" Danziger and Thad Eure, Jr.

With creativity and an innovative style for food service, Austrian-born Danziger catapulted Chapel Hill into the food leader of the Triangle pack. Franklin Street became his kingdom. Danziger owned and operated Zoom-Zoom, the Rathskeller, Ranch House and the magnificent Villa Teo—any of which would fit easily into the food-savvy Nineties.

Another illustrious name linked to the present state of the Triangle food scene is Thad Eure, Jr. who in the Sixties with then-partner Charles Winston built a barn-like structure on U.S. Highway 70 close to the airport. Folks scoffed at the idea of a restaurant "way out yonder" and predicted it would never work. It did.

Thad Eure, Jr. during his lifetime achieved national repute in the restaurant industry. And we in the Triangle shared his spotlight as The Angus Barn became one of the top-grossing restaurants in the country. The scoffers? They retreated long ago vanquished by a dream, a keen eye for real estate and a darn good steak.

The Triangle joined most of the nation in what is now known as the Food Revolution of the Seventies. Before then, Fowler's Grocery on Franklin Street in Chapel Hill and the thin rows of "gourmet" products in area grocery stores provided the only ammunition with which to upgrade our table.

Our ever-burgeoning food consciousness took full-wing in the latter half of the Seventies when Moreton and Bill Neal, discipled by that jolly messiah Julia Child, opened the original Restaurant La Residence in what is now Fearrington House located between Chapel Hill and Pittsboro.

The menu at La Residence presented classic French cuisine spilling toward Mediterranean: dense, buttery pates redolent with garlic and fresh green herbs and fresh mussels peeking open in a steamy broth.

Bill Neal went on to become a food writer with a folksy brilliant style that made him a nationally acclaimed culinarian. His books could well have been the beacon that drew the world to our Southern door, a world eager to hear the recipes of "Southernhood" rendered in imagined molasses drawls.

With the Eighties the stage was set. "Liquor-by-the-drink" became legal. Large hotels and convention complexes were erected. Research Triangle Park mushroomed, and our population was swelled by migrating Northerners lured by our pace, climate and job opportunities.

A new population brought new tastes and affluence, providing the perfect medium for restaurant growth both in scope and numbers. An industry of pride and creativity is now firmly entrenched in our local culture with so many fine talented men and women contributing daily to our communal table.

We writers in the Triangle who chronicle this diverse feast of ideas and substance are fortunate. We are never bored. And all of us greet the new millennium as an exciting proscenium to future imagination and food art with our "top chefs of the Triangle" as able guides.

Fred Benton is Food Editor of Spectator magazine. His radio shows, Food Forum and Food Forum's Better Living are aired on WDNC-620AM.

No project of this size is accomplished single-handedly, and *American Express Presents Top Chefs of the Triangle* is no exception. Throughout the process many people have helped to make this book a reality—some wittingly, some unknowing.

The concept for this project was born in the creative mind of Raleigh Magazine's publisher, Bob Dill. He has been the pilot and navigator, the engineer and chaplain, and oftentimes the friend who listened and made constructive suggestions as we brought this book from his dream to the reality you hold in your hand today.

As the recipes poured over the fax, came in through e-mail, or were deposited in the mail box, the test kitchen went into full swing. Gay Todd arrived each morning as bright and cheery as the Carolina sky. She chopped and diced, measured and mixed, steamed and sautéed but, most of all, she shared her sense of humor and made each test day go by in an organized flash.

I am especially grateful to good friend Fred Benton who was always available to help interpret a recipe, give insight on a chef, check the spelling of an ingredient, or just encourage me when the days got hot, and the kitchen hotter.

Hannaford's made the shopping on test days a pleasure. With few exceptions we were able to find every ingredient we needed. Beth Wyatt, fishmonger at Wellspring Grocery in Durham, was an invaluable source. Her knowledge of seafood is vast, and the fish she sells is strictly first class.

The exquisite photography in *Top Chefs* was painstakingly shot by professional photographer Michael Back. After knowledge and lighting you need to have food, props and an experienced stylist to make beautiful pictures. We want to extend particular gratitude to Karen Hough and Kellie Lewis at April Cornell in Crabtree Valley Mall for their generosity in lending us all the props we asked for. The tableware and fabrics at April Cornell are handsome and contribute a definite mood to the photography. The food, of course, was artfully prepared by each of the participating chefs, often at the most inconvenient times—and we extend a million thanks to each of them. The devil is in the details—and the photography stylist is the Vice President of Details. Our Vice President was Sandee Back, and you can see by the results what a beautiful job she did.

We didn't always have all the equipment we needed to test a recipe, but Executive Chef William D'Auvray and Pastry Chef Jacob Hartman, both of Cafe Giorgios, were always ready to furnish anything we needed. Chef William was tireless in a marathon session with the photographer to achieve the perfect presentation for our cover.

The recipe testing is long over, but our wonderful neighbors, willing guinea pigs all, are still talking about their favorite dishes. They lined up at the door, like hurricane refugees, with plastic containers out-stretched. While they lapped up the successes, the failures, and there were a few, were happily consumed by the gourmet gordon setter, Buckie.

Of course, a monumental "thank you" goes to the imaginative and talented men and women chefs in the Triangle who spend their life creating and preparing wonderful and innovative cuisine for our pleasure. Without them this book would not exist.

And finally, as with all my ventures, this project was undeniably enhanced by the constant support and involvement of David Thompson, my partner at table and in all of my life.

Jane Sears Thompson
Wake Forest, North Carolina

INTRODUCTION

▼

Raleigh, Durham and Chapel Hill, North Carolina are commonly called the "Triangle" because of their geographic proximity to each other. Each community has a rich, and separate history, culture and atmosphere. Those of us who live in the Triangle revel in their dissimilarities, and the opportunities and experiences those differences offer. But one of the common threads that runs throughout the region is the love of good food and fine dining. Our citizens and visitors alike can savor down-home barbecue one night, quenelles in a beurre blanc the next, and ginger-steamed sea bass with Thai mango salad the next— and travel less than 30 minutes to enjoy any of them.

American Express® Presents Top Chefs of the Triangle is a compendium of 270 recipes from 35 of our region's culinary stars. Each chef is an artist in his or her own right—selecting the raw materials freely and manipulating them according to the dictates of their creativity and talent.

Whether you're an armchair cook who loves to read recipes and look at beautiful pictures, a beginner in the kitchen, or a graduate of Le Cordon Bleu, there's something here for you.

The peanut butter pie from Red, Hot & Blue can be made in 5 minutes—plus a couple of hours of chilling, if you can wait that long. The spinach-stuffed grouper fillets wrapped in prosciutto from Il Palio Ristorante take only a few minutes to make, but their beauty will cause a hush in the dining room when you serve them. The creamy sweet onion soup from Lucky 32 is easy to prepare and perfect served with crusty French bread on a rainy evening. Go ahead. Turn the pages. Each recipe will cause your mouth to water.

We hope this book will inspire you to create great meals and share them with your family and friends. And, to drop by your favorite restaurant, or perhaps find a new favorite. Any of our Top Chefs would be delighted to entertain you.

From the editors at *Raleigh Magazine,* and each of our Top Chefs

Bon Appétit & Happy Cooking

Baby Back Ribs with Barbecue Sauce
Tomato Soup with Herbs

BETTY SHUGART
EXECUTIVE CHEF

The Angus Barn in Raleigh, one of the first Triangle restaurants to reap national attention, lives up to its slogan, "Beefeater's Haven." But seafood, baby back pork ribs and an extensive and award-winning wine list are other incentives that make "The Barn" popular.

▼▼▼▼▼▼▼▼▼▼▼▼▼▼▼▼▼▼▼▼▼▼▼▼▼▼▼▼▼

Tomato Soup with Herbs

2 Tablespoons sugar
1 Tablespoon butter
3 1/2 Cups chicken stock, divided
3 Cups tomato juice
1 1/2 Tablespoons tomato paste
1/2 teaspoon crushed garlic
1 1/2 teaspoons dried tarragon
1 teaspoon dried dill weed
2 Tablespoons white wine
2 Tablespoons cornstarch
2 teaspoons lemon juice
Salt and freshly ground black pepper
Sour cream, dill weed and garlic croutons
    for garnish

In a large uncovered pot melt butter and sugar over medium heat. When sugar has caramelized to a light brown add 2 1/2 cups chicken stock, tomato juice, tomato paste and garlic. Bring to boil, then immediately reduce to simmer.

In a small saucepan boil 1/2 cup chicken stock seasoned with tarragon and dill weed for 1 minute. Cover, and let steep for 2 minutes. Strain through fine-mesh strainer or cheesecloth, and add to simmering soup. Discard tarragon and dill weed.

In a small bowl blend remaining 1/2 cup chicken stock (cooled to room temperature, or cold) with wine and cornstarch. Whisk until well blended, and add to soup. Stir gently for 5 minutes or until soup is slightly thickened and cornstarch is thoroughly cooked. Season with lemon juice, salt and pepper. Garnish with sour cream, dill weed and toasted garlic croutons.

Smoked Bluefish Pasta Salad

1 pound penne pasta, cooked
12 ounces smoked bluefish (or smoked tuna)
6 Tablespoons olive oil
Balsamic vinegar to taste
1 Tablespoon chopped parsley
1 Tablespoon chopped cilantro leaves
1/2 Cup diced yellow bell pepper
1/2 Cup diced red bell pepper
1/2 Cup chopped red onion
1 1/2 Tablespoons soy sauce
Salt and freshly ground black pepper
Endive and lemon wedges for garnish

Pull the smoked fish into shreds, and mix all ingredients together. Garnish with endive and lemon wedges.

Baby Back Ribs with Barbecue Sauce

For the Barbecue Sauce

1 1/2 quarts cider vinegar
3/4 Cup Worcestershire sauce
2 teaspoons McCormick® barbecue spice
3/4 Cup ketchup
1 teaspoon salt
1/2 teaspoon finely chopped
    chili pepper pods
1/4 teaspoon chili powder
1/8 Cup mustard
1 Cup tomato juice
1 Tablespoon lemon juice
3/4 Cup brown sugar
1/4 Cup tarragon vinegar

In a deep, heavy-bottom saucepan combine all ingredients. Simmer for 45 minutes, but do not boil.

For the Ribs

Steam or parboil ribs in salted water until tender, about 20 minutes. Drain, and place ribs in a roasting pan. Cover with 2 cups barbecue sauce, and bake for 15 minutes at 350°F. Remove from oven and transfer ribs to a charcoal grill set over hot coals. Brush both sides of ribs with remaining sauce, and cook until golden brown. Brush very lightly with honey before removing from grill.

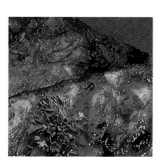

Potato Gratin

2 pounds Red Bliss potatoes, unpeeled
10 Tablespoons (1 stick + 2 Tablespoons)
    butter, softened
1 Cup sour cream
1/3 Cup bacon bits
1/3 Cup chopped chives
Salt and freshly ground black pepper
1/3 Cup grated Parmesan cheese

In lightly salted water boil potatoes until tender. Drain, and mash potatoes, but do not peel. Add remaining ingredients, except Parmesan, and mix well.

Spoon potato mixture into 6 single-serving casseroles. Top each with Parmesan, and bake in a 350°F oven until hot and lightly browned, about 25 minutes. Remove from oven, and brush top of each casserole with melted butter.

Chocolate Chess Pie

1 unbaked 9-inch pie shell
8 Tablespoons (1 stick) butter
2 squares (2 ounces) Baker's®
    semisweet chocolate
1 Cup sugar
2 eggs, beaten
1 1/2 teaspoons vanilla extract
Dash salt
Whipped cream for garnish

In the top of a double boiler over hot, not boiling, water melt butter and chocolate. Combine sugar, eggs, vanilla and salt, and add to chocolate. Stir until well blended. Pour into unbaked pie shell, and bake at 350°F for 50 minutes. Cool completely. Top with whipped cream.

Chilled Cucumber Soup
Southwest Seafood Salsa Salad
Crispy Calamari with Two Sauces

Anotherthyme Cuisine
Coffee and Spirits Bar

MARY S. BACON
CHEF-PROPRIETOR

Anotherthyme is another nationally acclaimed Triangle eatery. Located in the historic Brightleaf section of Durham, Anotherthyme's fare is multi-cultural with a decided accent on the American Southwest. Chef-proprietor Mary Bacon has presided over this gustatory landmark for over 20 years, consistently delivering well-balanced and artfully-presented cuisine.

▼▼▼▼▼▼▼▼▼▼▼▼▼▼▼▼▼▼▼▼▼▼▼▼▼
Chilled Cucumber Soup

For the Soup
8 Cups peeled, seeded and chopped
   cucumbers, divided
1 teaspoon salt
1 1/4 Cups chopped leeks
1 Cup chicken stock
1/4 Cup minced fresh spearmint
3 Cups tomato juice
2 teaspoons salt
3/4 teaspoon white pepper
4 Cups yogurt
1 1/2 Cups 2% milk
1 1/2 Cups buttermilk

In a colander set over a large bowl combine 7 cups chopped cucumbers with salt, allow to drain for 15 minutes. Rinse cucumbers well, and continue to drain. Reserve remaining cucumbers for garnish.

Boil leeks in chicken stock for 5 to 7 minutes. Add well-drained cucumbers to leeks and stock, and cook on medium-high heat for 4 minutes. Remove from heat, and add spearmint, tomato juice, salt and white pepper. Transfer mixture to a blender, and blend on high speed until very smooth. Cool. Transfer to a large bowl, and add yogurt, milk and buttermilk, and whisk gently until smooth.

For the Tomato Sauce
2 Tablespoons olive oil
3/4 Cups minced onion
2 Cups diced, peeled & seeded fresh tomatoes
1/2 teaspoon salt
1 Tablespoon chopped fresh basil
Pinch freshly ground black pepper

Sauté onions in olive oil for 5 minutes, and add remaining ingredients. Cook over low heat for 30 minutes. Remove from heat, and cool. When cool blend until very smooth. Funnel into plastic squirt bottle, and chill.

For the Seasoned Shrimp
6 Cups water
1 large bay leaf
1 Tablespoon dill seed
1 Tablespoon salt
1/2 teaspoon dried thyme
1/4 teaspoon cayenne pepper
1/4 Cup lemon juice
1/3 Cup dry white wine
1 pound (60/70 count) unpeeled shrimp

Combine all ingredients except shrimp in a large pot. Bring to a boil. Add shrimp, and reduce heat to simmer. When 3 or 4 shrimp rise to the top remove pot from heat. Drain immediately, and allow shrimp to cool. When shrimp are cool, peel and mince. Refrigerate until ready to use.

For the Garnish

    2 Tablespoons minced chives
    1/4 Cup spearmint chiffonade
      [See *Cook's Notes & Glossary*]

To Assemble

    Ladle soup into soup plates. Apply chilled tomato sauce in an "S" pattern through middle of soup. Add 1 heaping tablespoon chopped, seasoned shrimp in one curve of the S. Add 1 tablespoon of chopped cucumbers in the other curve of the S. Sprinkle minced chives on top of soup, and put a chiffonade of spearmint off center of the S. Serve immediately.

▼▼▼▼▼▼▼▼▼▼▼▼▼▼▼▼▼▼▼▼▼▼▼▼▼▼▼

Crispy Calamari with Two Sauces

For the Roasted Tomato Salsa

    5 medium-size tomatoes
    2 Tablespoons olive oil
    1/2 Cup minced onions
    1 bay leaf
    1 1/2 teaspoons salt
    1/4 teaspoon coarsely ground black pepper
    1/2 teaspoon minced fresh garlic
    1/2 teaspoon minced dried ancho chile
      [See *Editor's Note*]
    3/4 teaspoon ground cumin
    1 teaspoon ground coriander
    Pinch dried thyme
    2 teaspoons fresh oregano or marjoram
    1 teaspoon minced lime zest
    2 Tablespoons fresh lime juice
    1 teaspoon minced lemon zest
    1/2 Cup water

Wash tomatoes, and pat dry. Roast core side down on a medium hot grill or over open flame of a gas burner until half of each tomato is soft. Turn tomatoes over, and continue roasting until entire tomato is soft. Discard two thirds of skin, and chop remaining tomatoes and skin in a food processor. Do not puree.

    In a large skillet over medium-high heat add olive oil, then add onions, bay leaf, salt, pepper, garlic, ancho chile, cumin, coriander, thyme and oregano. Sauté mixture for 2 minutes over medium heat, then add roasted tomatoes, lime zest, lemon zest and lime juice. Add water as needed if mixture is too thick. Simmer 30 to 40 minutes, continuing to add water as needed.

For the Cilantro Mayonnaise

    1/3 Cup minced shallots
    1/2 Cup dry white wine
    1 teaspoon salt
    1/2 teaspoon dry mustard
    1/2 teaspoon white pepper
    Pinch cayenne pepper
    1 teaspoon ground coriander
    1 Cup Egg Beaters®
    3 Tablespoons fresh lime juice
    1 Cup vegetable oil
    1 Cup olive oil
    1/3 Cup chopped fresh cilantro leaves

In a sauté pan reduce wine with shallots until liquid is absorbed. Add salt, mustard, white pepper, cayenne and coriander. Sauté a few seconds and cool.

    Put Egg Beaters in a blender or food processor, and blend on low for 30 seconds. Add shallot mixture and lime juice. Blend for 10 seconds. With blender on low speed slowly drizzle oils into mixture. Add cilantro leaves. Blend for 20 seconds. Do not overblend or you may "burn" the cilantro and ruin the mayonnaise.

For the Calamari

    1 1/2 pounds frozen calamari, thawed
    1 Cup all-purpose flour
    2/3 Cup self-rising flour
    1/3 Cup yellow cornmeal
    1 1/2 teaspoons freshly ground black pepper
    1 Tablespoon salt
    Peanut oil for frying

Wash calamari, and cut into 1/4-inch rings. Keep wet. Mix remaining ingredients, except oil, in a plastic or paper bag.

    Pour 3 to 4 inches oil in a deep saucepan. Heat to 350°F. Shake off excess water from calamari rings, and place a handful of rings in bag with seasoned breading. Shake the bag. Remove calamari from bag, shake off excess breading, and put into hot fat. Cook for no more than 1 to 1 1/2 minutes. (Any longer and the calamari will become tough.) Remove calamari from fat with a slotted spoon, and place onto paper towels to drain. Continue until all calamari are cooked. Serve with the two sauces.

▼▼▼▼▼▼▼▼▼▼▼▼▼▼▼▼▼▼▼▼▼▼▼▼▼

Southwest Seafood Salsa Salad

    1 pound calamari, cut into rings
    1/2 pound bay scallops
    24 shrimp, shelled and deveined

For the Seafood Sauce

    2 Tablespoons butter, melted
    3/4 teaspoon minced garlic
    1 1/2 Tablespoons minced fresh ginger
    1 1/2 teaspoons salt
    1/2 teaspoon minced chipotle chili pepper
    1 teaspoon ground coriander
    1/4 Cup minced shallots
    2 Tablespoons lemon juice
    1/2 Cup fresh orange juice
    1 teaspoon minced lemon zest
    1/4 Cup Chardonnay wine
    3/4 Cup clam juice

Melt butter in a sauté pan over medium heat. When foam subsides add minced garlic, and cook for 1 minute. Combine remaining ingredients, and add to pan. Cook for 10 minutes. Add shrimp, and sauté about 2 minutes. (Shrimp should be almost, but not completely, cooked.) Remove shrimp from pan, and reserve. Add scallops, and cook 1 minute. Remove, and reserve. Cook calamari rings for 1 minute. Remove. Combine shrimp, scallops and calamari, and refrigerate.

For the Salsa

    2 Cups minced tomatoes
    2 Cups peeled and minced cucumbers
    1 Cup minced red onion
    2 Tablespoons minced jalapeño pepper
    3 Cups shoepeg corn, steamed for 4 minutes
    3/4 Cup lime juice
    1/2 Cup orange juice
    1 1/2 teaspoons salt
    3/4 teaspoon freshly ground black pepper
    1 1/2 teaspoons sugar
    1/4 Cup pure olive oil

Combine all ingredients, and toss well. Refrigerate. When cool combine with cooked seafood, and serve.

▼▼▼▼▼▼▼▼▼▼▼▼▼▼▼▼▼▼▼▼▼▼▼▼▼▼

Double Chocolate Cake

For the Cake

    1/2 Cup water
    8 ounces premium bittersweet chocolate
    1 1/2 Cups all-purpose flour
    1 1/8 teaspoons baking soda
    3/4 teaspoon baking powder
    Pinch salt
    7 Tablespoons salted butter
    1 Cup sugar
    4 eggs, separated

    1 1/2 teaspoons vanilla extract
    1 Cup buttermilk
    1 Cup sugar

Coarsely chop chocolate, and combine with water in a saucepan. Heat over low heat, stirring until chocolate is melted and smooth. Set aside.

Sift dry ingredients together, and set aside. Using an electric mixer, beat butter and sugar at low speed until smooth, about 5 minutes. Add egg yolks, one at a time, and beat until well mixed. Do not overmix. Add chocolate and vanilla. Mix just to combine. Add buttermilk and flour, and mix on low speed 2 minutes until fully incorporated. Using a rubber spatula scrape sides of bowl, and set aside.

Beat 3 egg whites until stiff, but not dry. Gently fold whites into batter. Pour batter into 2 9-inch greased and floured cake pans. Bake at 350°F for 50 minutes or until a toothpick inserted in the center comes out clean. Cool layers for several hours before icing.

For the Icing

    12 ounces bittersweet chocolate
    1 1/4 Cups powdered (10X) sugar
    1 1/2 Cups (3 sticks) softened butter
    6 egg yolks, at room temperature
    1/3 Cup dark rum, such as Myers's®
    1/4 Cup hot water
    2 teaspoons vanilla extract

Coarsely chop chocolate, and melt in top of double boiler or bowl placed over hot water. Using an electric mixer, cream butter and sugar on low speed until smooth, approximately 5 minutes. Add egg yolks, one at a time, incorporating each yolk before adding the next. Scrape sides of bowl often. Add hot water, rum, vanilla, and beat until smooth. Add chocolate, and beat on low speed until thoroughly blended, approximately 1 minute. Increase speed to medium, and beat for 10 minutes until mixture is dark and shiny and slightly thickened.

Ice bottom cake layer with one third of icing. Place next layer on top and ice top and sides with remaining icing. Refrigerate.

Editor's Note

   • Tomatoes can also be roasted by cutting them in half horizontally, placing them skin side down on a baking sheet, drizzling 1/2 teaspoon olive oil and a liberal sprinkling of salt and pepper on the cut side of each tomato half, and roasting them in a 350°F oven for 30 to 45 minutes, or until the edges turn a crusty brown.

   • Ancho chilies must be softened by soaking in water for 5 to 10 minutes before mincing and measuring.

Mixed Fish Grill with Orange Olive Sauce

**GWEN HIGGINS
EXECUTIVE CHEF**

Aurora in Carrboro was the Triangle's pioneer in Northern Italian cuisine and pasta presentations. The late-afternoon crowd strolling through Carr Mill Mall is often lured to Aurora's door by the heady aroma of fresh bread baking. Bread is a particular passion of chef Gwen Higgins.

▼▼▼▼▼▼▼▼▼▼▼▼▼▼▼▼▼▼▼▼▼▼▼▼▼▼▼▼

Zuppa Santa
(Potato and Leek Soup)

4 potatoes, peeled and cubed
4 large leeks, white part only,
  coarsely chopped
2 onions, coarsely chopped
2 celery ribs, coarsely chopped
6 Cups boiling water
1 teaspoon salt
2 Tablespoons butter
1 Cup heavy cream
1/4 teaspoon white pepper
1 Tablespoon salt
1/2 teaspoon vinegar
3 Tablespoons lemon juice
1/2 teaspoon freshly ground black pepper
2 Tablespoons chopped chives for garnish

Cover all vegetables with 6 cups, lightly salted, boiling water. Cover pot, and simmer for 30 minutes until vegetables are tender. Drain, and reserve liquid.

In a food processor or blender, puree cooked vegetables in batches. Add cooking liquid, butter and cream. Pulse on and off. Add white pepper, salt, vinegar, lemon juice and black pepper. Pulse on and off to incorporate. Pour into bowls, sprinkle with chives and serve. This soup is also delicious cold.

Marinated Scallops

3 pounds sea scallops
1/4 Cup minced onion
1/2 Cup minced hard-boiled egg
1/2 Cup minced parsley
1 Tablespoon relish
1 1/2 Cups olive oil
2 1/4 Cups white vinegar
2 teaspoons salt
1/2 teaspoon pepper
1/4 teaspoon crushed fresh garlic
1/4 teaspoon dried basil
2 heads leaf lettuce
Lemon wedges for garnish

Parboil scallops in boiling water for 45 seconds. Remove, drain, rinse with cold water and reserve.

Combine remaining ingredients in a non-reactive bowl. Add cooled scallops, and marinate for 6 to 8 hours.

Serve on a bed of lettuce garnished with lemon wedges.

Mixed Fish Grill with Orange Olive Sauce

6 fish steaks, such as salmon,
    sea bass or swordfish (6-ounce each)
1/4 Cup peanut oil
3 Tablespoons tamari soy sauce
1/2 teaspoon minced garlic

Combine oil, soy sauce and garlic in a non-reactive dish. Place fish in marinade, cover and refrigerate for 4 to 24 hours, turning the fish occasionally.

Grill marinated fish steaks to desired doneness. Serve topped with sauce.

For the Sauce

1 Cup sherry vinegar
2 Cups fresh orange juice
1/2 Cup walnut oil
1/2 Cup peanut oil
1/2 teaspoon orange zest
1 teaspoon chopped fresh rosemary
1 teaspoon chopped fresh chives
1 teaspoon salt
1/2 teaspoon freshly ground black pepper
6 kalamata olives, pitted

In a small saucepan over high heat combine sherry vinegar and orange juice, and reduce to 1/2 cup. As liquid reduces and thickens stir constantly to avoid burning. Resulting liquid will have the consistency of syrup.

Remove syrup from heat, and pour into a blender container. Set blender speed on low, and slowly add walnut and peanut oils in a steady stream. When mixture is thickened transfer to a bowl, and stir in remaining ingredients.

Fruit Filled Meringues

8 egg whites, at room temperature
Dash cream of tartar
1 1/4 Cups sugar
1 Tablespoon Galliano® liqueur (or Pernod®)
1 1/2 Tablespoons grenadine syrup
4 Tablespoons cornstarch
2 Tablespoons orange zest,
    blanched in boiling water and chopped

Line a baking sheet with parchment paper. Grease and lightly flour the paper.

Using an electric mixer on medium speed beat egg whites until foamy. Add cream of tartar, and increase speed to high. Continue beating while adding sugar gradually. Beat for 5 minutes until very stiff peaks form. Reduce mixer speed to medium, and add liqueur, grenadine, cornstarch and zest. Return speed to high, and beat for 3 minutes. Peaks should be very stiff.

Using a pastry bag with large star tip pipe meringue onto prepared parchment paper making a flat circular base about 2 1/2 inches in diameter. Form a cup by piping 2 layers around outer edge of circle. Repeat process to make 5 more meringues. Bake at 350°F for 10 minutes. Lower heat to 225°F, and continue baking for 1 hour or until meringues are very dry. Turn oven off and, if desired, leave meringues in oven overnight to ensure complete dryness. Store in air-tight container.

For the Filling
3 Cups fresh fruit, such as blueberries,
    raspberries or peaches
2 Tablespoons lemon juice
1/3 Cup sugar
1/4 Cup port
1 Cup heavy cream, whipped (optional)
6 mint leaves for garnish

In a non-reactive bowl combine lemon juice, sugar and port. Add fruit, and gently toss. Cover, and allow to marinate in refrigerator for 1 to 24 hours.

Just before serving spoon fruit into meringue cups. Top each with whipped cream and mint leaf.

Cheese Cake

For the Graham Cracker Crust
5 Tablespoons butter, melted
1 Tablespoon sugar
1 Cup graham cracker crumbs

Spray inside of an 8-inch springform pan with vegetable oil spray. Line with plastic wrap to keep water bath from seeping in and ruining the cake. For extra protection place pan in middle of a large piece of aluminum foil, and wrap foil up and around the outside of the pan.

Combine butter, sugar and graham cracker crumbs and press into bottom of the lined springform pan.

For the Filling
2 pounds cream cheese, at room temperature
5 ounces mascarpone cheese
5 eggs
1 1/2 Cups sugar
3 teaspoons vanilla extract
1 Tablespoon lemon juice
1/3 Cup heavy cream

Using an electric mixer on medium speed combine cheeses, and beat to smoothness for 1 to 2 minutes. Add 3 eggs, and mix thoroughly, taking care to scrape sides of bowl as needed. Add remaining eggs, and mix on low speed for 30 seconds. Using a wire whisk blend in sugar, vanilla, lemon juice and cream.

Pour filling into prepared springform pan. Place pan in large vessel, such as roaster or broiler pan that is at least 2 inches deep. Pour boiling water into roaster, being careful not to splash any water into cake batter. Water should come 1 to 1 1/2 inches up side of springform pan. Place on center rack of 350°F oven, and bake for 65 minutes. Top should be slightly brown, and middle should still jiggle. Cool on cake rack.

Cuban Pork Taco Salad
Linguine Mykonos

Black Dog Cafe and Backyard Bar

**CHEFS
SUE STEZICK
AND
HARVEY YANCEY**

The decor of the Black Dog Cafe and Backyard Bar is a dog-lover's paradise. Photographs of man's best friend depicting every shape, size and breed are displayed in the bar. The human palate ranks first, however, at the Black Dog where crowds of Raleigh's City Market habitues gather for lunch, dinner and late evenings.

Chicken Chili

2 pounds boneless, skinless chicken
    cut into 1/2-inch cubes
2 Tablespoons oil
2 Cups chopped onion
2 teaspoons minced garlic
1 can (4 1/2-ounce) chopped green chilies,
    drained
2 Cups cooked pinto beans
1 Cup chicken stock
1 teaspoon salt
1/2 teaspoon freshly ground black pepper
1/4 teaspoon cayenne pepper
2/3 Cup chopped fresh cilantro leaves
1 can (14 1/2-ounce) stewed tomatoes
2 Tablespoons chili powder
1 Tablespoon ground cumin
1/2 teaspoon oregano
1/4 Cup chopped sun-dried tomatoes
1 Cup grated Cheddar cheese
Whole cilantro leaves for garnish

In a large Dutch oven sauté chicken in oil for 5 minutes. Add onion and garlic, and continue to cook until chicken is lightly browned. Add remaining ingredients in the order given, except the cheese, and bring to a boil. Reduce heat to low, and simmer for at least 30 minutes.

Top with grated Cheddar cheese, and garnish with cilantro leaves.

Artichoke Spinach Dip

2 packages frozen chopped spinach
    (10-ounces each)
1 Cup ricotta cheese
1/2 Cup grated Parmesan cheese
1 Cup mayonnaise
1 Tablespoon minced garlic
1 can artichoke hearts (14-ounces),
    drained and coarsely chopped
2 teaspoons salt
1 teaspoon freshly ground black pepper

Thaw spinach, and squeeze out excess moisture.
In a mixing bowl combine remaining ingredients.
Add spinach, and stir until mixed. Spoon mixture
into a greased oven-proof casserole, and bake for
25 to 30 minutes at 350°F or until lightly browned.
Serve warm with water crackers.

Linguine Mykonos
(Linguine with Shellfish)

2 pounds linguine
3 Tablespoons olive oil
3 teaspoons minced garlic
2 Cups white wine
1/2 pound shrimp, peeled and deveined
1/2 pound sea scallops
4 Cups seeded, diced ripe tomatoes
25-30 kalamata olives, pitted
1/2 teaspoon crushed red pepper flakes
1/2 Cup chopped scallions
Salt and freshly ground black pepper
2 teaspoons chopped parsley
1/2 Cup crumbled feta cheese

Cook pasta according to package instructions.
Rinse with cool water, and set aside.

Heat olive oil in a large skillet over high heat.
Add garlic, and cook until lightly brown. Add
wine, and reduce by half. Add shrimp and scallops, and sauté for 45 seconds. Add tomatoes,
olives, red pepper flakes and scallions, and continue stirring until seafood is firm to the touch. Add
salt and pepper to taste, then add pasta. Toss gently until pasta is heated. Divide evenly among 6
pasta bowls, and top each presentation with
crumbled cheese and parsley.

Cuban Pork Taco Salad

2 1/2 teaspoons jerk seasoning
    [See Cook's Notes & Glossary]
1/2 teaspoon angostura bitters
1/2 Cup cider vinegar
2 1/2 pounds pork loin
2 Tablespoons olive oil
1/2 Cup chicken stock
2 teaspoons ground cumin
2 Tablespoons chili powder
2 Tablespoons salt
1 red bell pepper, seeded and diced
1 green bell pepper, seeded and diced
1 Cup diced onion
2 teaspoons minced garlic
1 Cup diced roma (plum) tomatoes
1/2 Cup chopped cilantro leaves
1/2 Cup chopped green chili peppers
6 10-inch flour tortillas
Vegetable oil for frying
1 head lettuce, finely chopped
2 Cups crushed corn chips
12 ounces grated Cheddar cheese
2 avocados, peeled and sliced
    just before using
1/2 Cup sliced black olives
1 Cup diced tomatoes
1 Cup sour cream
1 1/2 Cups cooked black beans

Add jerk seasoning and angostura bitters to vinegar. Pour mixture over pork, and toss to coat. Marinate for 20 to 30 minutes.

Heat olive oil in a large sauté pan. Add pork, and sauté until medium rare. Add chicken stock, cumin, chili powder and salt, and simmer for 10 to 15 minutes until liquid is reduced by half. Add peppers, onion, garlic, tomatoes, cilantro and chilies. Simmer until vegetables are tender.

Heat vegetable oil in a deep frying pan to 350°F. Place a 10-inch flour tortilla in the hot oil, and press a 6-inch skillet in middle of the tortilla so that sides of tortilla come up around sides of skillet, and the tortilla takes on the shape of a bowl. Fry until crisp. Remove tortilla from oil, and allow to drain well before use.

In the tortilla "bowl" layer lettuce, crushed corn chips, pork mixture, grated cheese, more lettuce, and top with diced tomatoes, avocado slices, sour cream, olives and black beans.

Double Chocolate Cake

3 eggs
3 Cups sugar
3/4 Cup vegetable oil
1 1/2 Cups buttermilk
1 Cup unsweetened cocoa powder
1 1/2 Cups boiling water
2 teaspoons baking soda
1 1/4 teaspoons baking powder
1 Tablespoon vanilla extract
2 1/2 Cups all-purpose flour
1 teaspoon salt

Using an electric mixer combine eggs, sugar, oil and buttermilk, and beat on medium-high speed for 1 minute, scraping the sides of the bowl as needed. Add cocoa, and mix on low speed for 30 seconds or until fully incorporated. Add boiling water, and mix for 1 minute. Add soda, baking powder and vanilla, and mix for 30 seconds. Add flour, and beat on medium speed for 3 minutes.

Pour batter into 2 greased 9-inch cake pans, and bake for 30 minutes at 350°F or until a knife inserted in the center comes out clean.

For the Icing
1 1/2 Cups (3 sticks) butter
1 pound powdered (10X) sugar
4 Tablespoons vanilla extract
1/2 Cup milk
8 ounces unsweetened chocolate, melted

Using an electric mixer on medium-high speed beat butter until smooth. Reduce speed to low, and slowly add powdered sugar, and blend well. Add vanilla, milk and melted chocolate, and blend until smooth. Ice cake only after it has completely cooled.

Pecan-Crusted Salmon with Oven-Roasted Potatoes and Green Beans

Bloomsbury Bistro

JOHN TOLER
CHEF-PROPRIETOR

The kitchen at Bloomsbury Bistro in Raleigh's Five Points area is directed by chef-proprietor John Toler. Both "Bon Appétit" magazine and New York's James Beard House have discovered John's talent for creating simple but concentrated flavors presented in a stylish and sophisticated manner.

Grilled Summer Zucchini and Vidalia Onion Vichyssoise

For the Crème Fraîche
> 2 Cups heavy cream
> 1/4 Cup buttermilk

Combine heavy cream and buttermilk in a 1-quart container. Shake vigorously for 60 seconds, and set aside for 24 hours. Cream will turn thick, almost the consistency of sour cream (which can be used as a substitute in a pinch).

For the Soup
> 2 pounds small zucchini
> 2 Tablespoons olive oil
> Salt and freshly ground black pepper
> 1 pound Vidalia onions, sliced
> 1 Tablespoon butter
> 1/2 pound russet potatoes, peeled and diced
> 3 Cups chicken stock
> 2 teaspoons salt
> 1 Cup heavy cream
> 2 Tablespoons chopped fresh dill
> 1/4 teaspoon Tabasco® Sauce
> 3 Tablespoons fresh lemon juice
> Sprigs of fresh dill for garnish

Cut zucchini into 1/4-inch vertical slices, and brush each slice with olive oil, and sprinkle with salt and pepper. Grill over high heat until tender. Don't allow skins to color too much or they will make the soup an undesirable shade of green. Once cooked, coarsely chop squash, and set aside.

In a large saucepan over medium heat melt butter, and slowly cook onions until transparent. Add chopped squash, potatoes, chicken stock and

2 teaspoons salt. Bring to boil, and simmer for 15 minutes or until potatoes are cooked through. Add heavy cream and return to boil. Immediately remove from heat, and liquify soup in blender. Refrigerate until cool.

Before serving, stir in fresh dill, Tabasco, lemon juice, and adjust salt and pepper. Serve in chilled bowls with a dollop of crème fraîche and additional sprigs of dill.

▼▼▼▼▼▼▼▼▼▼▼▼▼▼▼▼▼▼▼▼▼▼▼▼▼▼▼▼▼

Wilted Spinach Salad

For the Vinaigrette
    4 Tablespoons finely minced shallots
    1 Tablespoon chopped fresh thyme
    1/2 Cup cider vinegar
    1 Tablespoon Dijon mustard
    3 Tablespoons honey
    1/3 Cup peanut oil
    Salt and freshly ground black pepper
Place shallots, thyme and vinegar in a small saucepan, and cook over high heat until liquid is reduced by half. Use a wire whisk to stir in mustard and honey. Continue to whisk while adding oil in a slow, steady stream. Add salt and pepper to taste.

For the Salad
    1 1/2 pounds fresh spinach leaves,
       well cleaned
    1 Cup croutons
    1 Cup crisp-cooked, crumbled
       applewood smoked bacon
    1 Cup finely chopped red onion
    1 Cup finely diced smoked Gouda cheese
    1 pint cherry tomatoes, cut into quarters
Place spinach and croutons in a large heat-proof salad bowl. Combine vinaigrette with crumbled bacon and red onion. Heat mixture to boiling, then immediately pour hot vinaigrette over greens. Toss to wilt, and portion salad onto 6 plates. Sprinkle each with Gouda cheese, and garnish with cherry tomatoes.

▼▼▼▼▼▼▼▼▼▼▼▼▼▼▼▼▼▼▼▼▼▼▼▼▼▼▼▼▼

Pecan-Crusted Salmon with Oven-Roasted Potatoes and Green Beans

For the Potatoes
    2 pounds small red new potatoes, quartered
    1 teaspoon finely minced garlic
    3 Tablespoons olive oil
    2 Tablespoons chopped fresh thyme,
    Salt and freshly ground black pepper

Place potatoes, garlic, olive oil and thyme in a large flat roasting pan or baking sheet. Toss vegetables to coat evenly, then generously sprinkle with salt and pepper. Roast in a 350°F oven for about 25 minutes or until potatoes are crisp and can be easily pierced with a fork.

For the Beans
    2 quarts water
    1 Tablespoon salt
    1 pound green beans, tips removed
Blanch beans in boiling salted water for 3 to 4 minutes. Do not overcook. Rinse under cold water to restore bright green color. Drain well. Toss with potatoes, and set aside.

For the Salmon
    6 salmon fillets (6-ounce each)
       skinned and boned
    Salt and freshly ground black pepper
    2 Tablespoons peanut oil
    16 Tablespoons (2 sticks) butter, softened
    1 Cup coarsely chopped pecans
    1 Tablespoon chopped fresh thyme
    1/4 Cup lemon juice
    2 Tablespoons chopped Italian parsley
    6 Tablespoons capers, drained
Sprinkle salmon with salt and pepper. Heat a non-stick, oven-proof skillet until hot. Add peanut oil. When oil is hot place fillets in pan flesh side down. Sauté fish for 1 minute. Carefully flip fillets over, and turn off heat.

Brush fillets with some softened butter. Coat buttered side of each fillet with chopped pecans, and sprinkle thyme over nuts. Place fillets in a pre-heated 450°F oven and cook for 4 to 5 minutes or until fish is almost opaque throughout, and nuts have browned. Remove from oven and set aside while you make the sauce (the fish will continue to cook while standing).

Wipe out pan in which you cooked the fish. Place pan over high heat, and add remaining soft butter. Cook butter until it begins to bubble and starts to brown, about 2 minutes. When butter is brown and starts to smell like hazelnuts, remove skillet from heat, and add lemon juice. Shake pan to evenly distribute lemon juice. Stir in capers and chopped parsley. Adjust seasoning.

To Assemble
Mound potatoes and beans in center of each plate. Place a fish fillet on top, and drizzle brown butter over and around salmon. Serve at once.

Orzo Risotto with Grilled Vegetables

For the Grilled Vegetables

    1 medium zucchini, sliced lengthwise
    1 yellow squash, sliced lengthwise
    1 large red onion, sliced into
        1/4-inch thick slices
    1 eggplant, peeled, and sliced into
        1/4-inch thick slices
    1 large tomato, sliced into
        1/4-inch thick slices
    Pure olive oil for grilling
    1 Cup cooked fresh corn kernels

Brush sliced vegetables with pure olive oil. Generously salt and pepper vegetables, and grill over high heat. Vegetables should be slightly under-cooked because they will be reheated with the pasta. Allow vegetables to cool, then cut them into uniform pieces. Combine with fresh corn kernels, and set aside.

For the Marinade

    1 Cup extra virgin olive oil
    1/4 Cup red wine vinegar
    2 teaspoons minced garlic
    3 Tablespoons chopped fresh basil

Combine marinade ingredients in blender. Blend on medium-high speed until well combined.

To Complete the Dish

    6 slices French bread (1/8-inches thick)
    2 Cups cooked orzo pasta, drained and
        tossed with 1 Tablespoon olive oil
    2 Tablespoons chopped fresh thyme
    1 Cup chicken stock
    1 Cup freshly grated Parmesan cheese,
        plus extra for garnish
    1/3 Cup butter

Brush bread on both sides with some marinade. Grill until toasted, and set aside.

In a large heavy-bottom pot over medium-high heat, warm vegetables and orzo with stock and fresh thyme. Stir constantly and gently to prevent sticking. Once ingredients are hot, stir in butter and cheese. Continue stirring until cheese and butter are melted and mixture has a creamy consistency. Serve immediately with crostini and additional grated cheese.

Pistachio-Crusted Chocolate Terrine With Raspberry Coulis

    8 ounces Belgian semisweet chocolate,
        coarsely chopped
    1 Cup heavy cream, chilled
    2 teaspoons unflavored gelatin softened
        in 1 Tablespoon warm water
    1/2 Cup sugar, divided
    2 egg whites
    2 egg yolks
    1 Cup toasted, chopped pistachio nuts

Add chocolate to metal bowl placed over pot of simmering water. Stir occasionally until chocolate is barely melted. While chocolate is melting whip cream to soft peak stage. Add softened gelatin to cream, and whip to stiff peaks. Set aside.

Lightly mix egg whites with 1/4 cup sugar, and warm over simmering water until sugar is dissolved. Remove from heat, and whip to stiff peaks. Set aside.

Beat yolks with remaining 1/4 cup sugar until mixture is very thick and light yellow in color. Set aside.

Line a rectangular 6-cup loaf pan with plastic wrap (this will allow you to easily unmold the terrine).The success of this dessert relies on working quickly from this point on. Have all prepared ingredients within easy reach, and do not overmix during the different stages.

Using a whisk gently stir yolk mixture into chocolate until blended, then gently incorporate egg whites. Be very delicate so volume is not lost. Use a broad rubber spatula to fold in whipped cream. Spoon mixture into prepared mold, and refrigerate at least 3 hours or until terrine is set and firm to the touch. You can prepare terrine up to 3 days before serving.

For the Raspberry Coulis

    1 Cup fresh or frozen raspberries
    1/3 Cup fresh lemon juice
    4 Tablespoons sugar

Place berries, lemon juice and sugar in a blender, and liquify on high speed. Pour through fine-mesh strainer. Taste for sweetness, and adjust if necessary.

To Assemble

Unmold terrine. Dip a knife into very hot water before cutting each of 6 equal slices. Place each slice on a plate, and coat top with chopped pistachios. Drizzle raspberry coulis over and around terrine, and serve at once with whipped cream on the side.

Pan-Crisped Halibut Over Thai Mango Salad

Cafe Giorgios

Cafe Giorgios is a reflection of the flamboyance of its Mediterranean namesake Giorgios Bakatsias. The cuisine draws from executive chef William D'Auvray's French heritage and Asian upbringing. Both combine to create a varied and exciting menu at this popular North Raleigh gathering spot.

GIORGIOS BAKATSIAS (STANDING) AND WILLIAM D'AUVRAY, EXECUTIVE CHEF

Warm Duck Salad

For the Vinaigrette
> 1/4 Cup chopped chives or scallions
> 1 ounce Chinese fermented black beans, rinsed well [See *Editor's Note*]
> 1/4 cup rice wine vinegar
> 2 Tablespoons minced candied ginger
> 2 Tablespoons pure olive oil
> 1 Thai chili, minced
> 1 Tablespoon brown sugar

Process black beans and candied ginger into a paste. Combine in a bowl with remaining ingredients, and set aside.

For the Salad
> 4 Cups duck confit [See *Editor's Note*]
> 1 pound angel hair pasta
> 1/2 pound arugula leaves, stems removed
> 4 leeks, white part only
> 1/2 Cup unbleached bread flour
> 2 1/4 Cups peanut oil, divided
> 1 teaspoon sesame oil

Pour a third of vinaigrette over duck confit. Marinate for 2 hours in refrigerator or for 30 minutes at room temperature.

For Noodle Cakes
Cook angel hair pasta in boiling, salted water according to package directions. When cooked, rinse pasta under running cold water, and drain completely. Toss pasta with 1 tablespoon peanut oil and 1 teaspoon sesame oil. Wrapping pasta around your index and middle fingers, make 6 pasta balls. Use palms of your hands to flatten balls into 1-inch thick cakes. Reserve.

Discard green tops from leeks, and cut white part into 2 1/2-inch sections. Cut into thin julienne strips. Place leeks in ice water, and reserve.

To a cast iron skillet over medium heat add 3 tablespoons peanut oil. When oil is hot sauté each noodle cake until golden brown and crispy. Drain on paper towels, and reserve.

For the Crispy Leeks
Heat 2 cups peanut oil in small saucepan. While oil is heating to 350°F drain leeks, dry and toss in flour. Shake off excess flour, and fry in hot oil until leeks are light golden in color. Do not brown.

To Assemble
Place a noodle cake in center of each of 6 large dinner plates. Toss arugula leaves in half of remaining vinaigrette, and place a handful of arugula on top of each noodle cake. Place a portion of pickled, marinated duck on top of arugula. Top duck with crispy leeks, and drizzle remaining vinaigrette around edges of salad. Garnish with chopped chives.

Pan-Crisped Halibut
Over Thai Mango Salad

For the Halibut
        2 3/4 pounds fresh halibut fillets
        3 Tablespoons peanut oil
        1/2 teaspoon butter
        3 teaspoons salt
        1/2 teaspoon freshly ground black pepper
        1/4 teaspoon cayenne pepper
Have the fishmonger skin and fillet halibut, and cut into 6 equal portions. Season each portion with salt, black pepper and cayenne pepper.

Heat peanut oil in large iron skillet over medium-high heat. Add butter. When foam subsides add halibut fillets flesh side (not skin side) down. Do not move fillets or agitate pan for 3 to 4 minutes. When fillets start to brown around the edges, carefully turn them over, and cook for 1 minute on skin side. Place fillets on a platter while you discard used oil and butter. Return fillets to pan, but do not heat pan. As you prepare leeks, the fish will continue to cook.

For the Mango Salad
        6 green mangoes, peeled, seeded
            and thinly sliced
        1 Cup sugar
        2 1/2 ounces fish sauce [See *Editor's Note*]
        3/4 Cup minced scallions
        1/4 Cup chopped fresh mint
        2 Tablespoons lemon juice
        2 Tablespoons Thai Chili Oil (recipe below)
Place mango slices in large mixing bowl. Sprinkle with sugar, and let stand for 5 minutes. With a wooden spoon stir vigorously until sugar dissolves, almost smashing mango slices. Add remaining ingredients, stir to combine, and reserve.

For the Roasted Curry-Citrus Vinaigrette
        1 1/2 Cups fresh orange juice
        1/3 Cup fresh lime juice
        1/2 Cup fresh lemon juice
        1/2 Cup Thai curry powder
            [See *Editor's Note*]
        1/2 Cup tightly packed light brown sugar
        1/4 Cup chopped fresh basil
        1 teaspoon fish sauce [See *Editor's Note*]
        1/2 Cup vegetable oil
        1/4 Cup extra virgin olive oil

Mix citrus juices, curry powder and brown sugar in large mixing bowl until sugar dissolves. Add fresh basil and fish sauce and stir. Blend olive oil and vegetable oil together, and whisking constantly pour into citrus mixture.

For the Thai Chili Oil
        5 Thai chilies
        1 Cup extra virgin olive oil
Warm oil, add chilies. Cover and let steep for at least 30 minutes. Strain to remove chilies, and reserve oil.

For Crispy Leeks
        Follow recipe on page 39.

To Assemble
        Spoon a portion of mango salad onto each plate. Top with halibut fillet and crispy leeks. Drizzle vinaigrette around fish, and serve.

Ginger-Steamed Flounder
with Three-Flavored Broth

        1 whole flounder (3- to 4-pounds), cleaned
            and gills removed
        1 bunch scallions cut into 2-inch pieces
        1/4 Cup coarsely chopped
            fresh cilantro leaves
        1 Cup fresh lime juice
        1/2 Cup julienned ginger root
        2 lime leaves [See *Editor's Note*]
        1 Tablespoon fish sauce [See *Editor's Note*]
        3 Tablespoons kosher salt
        1 Tablespoon freshly ground black pepper
        3 Thai chilies [See *Editor's Note*]
        2 Tablespoons olive oil
        1 cucumber, peeled, seeded and julienned
        1 Cup dry white wine
        2 Cups water
        1 Cup julienned carrots
        1 1/2 Cups julienned leeks
Rinse flounder thoroughly, removing any blood trapped in the spine. Pat fish dry with paper towels. Make 4 to 6 vertical slices, cutting to the bone, on top and bottom of fish. Place fish in a large Pyrex® dish or deep heat-proof glass plate. Rub salt and pepper over fish, and place scallions, cilantro, lime juice, ginger, lime leaves, fish sauce,

Thai chilies and olive oil over and around fish. Cover, and refrigerate for 2 hours.

Pour water and wine into large steamer, and bring to a boil. Place dish with fish in steamer. Cover steamer, and cook fish for 10 minutes. Remove cover, and brush aromatics off top of fish and into plate with juices. Mix julienned cucumber, leeks and carrots together, and spread over top of fish. Replace steamer cover, and cook for 5 minutes.

For the Ginger Glaze
  1 Cup brown sugar
  1/2 Cup honey
  1/2 Cup finely chopped fresh ginger
  1/4 Cup olive oil
  1/2 Cup orange juice
  1 red bell pepper, seeded and finely diced
  1/2 Cup fresh lime juice
  Scallion flowers and cilantro sprigs
      for garnish

Place all ingredients except olive oil and lime juice into a small saucepan, and bring to a boil. Turn heat off, and cool. Whisk in olive oil, and set aside.

To Assemble
Remove fish from steamer, and place on a large, oval platter with a deep well. Just before serving combine a small amount of liquid from steamer with lime juice, and ladle over fish.

Drizzle with Ginger Glaze, and garnish with scallion flowers and cilantro.

Sticky Rice Pudding

  1 Cup Japanese-short grain rice, rinsed well
  3 1/2 Cups milk
  2 Tablespoons orange zest
  1 vanilla bean
  1 Cup sugar
  5 egg yolks
  7 Tablespoons butter
  1 3/4 teaspoons gelatin
  1 cinnamon stick
  1 Tablespoon cold water
  1/2 Cup brown sugar
  1 Cup heavy cream

Place rinsed rice in non-reactive saucepan. Cover with water, and bring to a boil. Cook over moderate heat for 4 minutes. Drain.

Put milk, orange zest, vanilla bean, sugar and cinnamon in saucepan, and add blanched rice. Bring to boil, cover, and reduce to simmer. Simmer for 25 minutes or until rice is tender and all but a small amount of liquid is absorbed.

Using an electric mixer cream butter and egg yolks together, and whisk into rice mixture. Add heavy cream, and continue to cook rice until mixture has thickened. Remove vanilla bean and cinnamon stick, and discard. Soften gelatin with cold water, and incorporate into rice. Divide rice pudding among individual souffle cups, and refrigerate for 2 hours or until set.

Editor's Note
• *Duck confit is available at gourmet stores or by mail order from D'Artagnan (1-800-DARTAGNAN—1-800-327-8246).*
• *Thai chilies, Thai curry powder, lime leaves and Chinese fermented black beans are available at several area Asian markets.*

Grilled Lamb with Eggplant and Roasted Onion-Red Pepper Relish
Grilled Lobster Salad with Citrus Vinaigrette

Cafe Parizade

Chef Robert Adams dishes up delectable Mediterranean cuisine at this Giorgios Bakatsias restaurant in Durham. Often touted as one of the prettiest restaurants in the Triangle, Parizade is usually packed with a fun-loving, food-loving crowd.

GIORGIOS BAKATSIAS CHEF-PROPRIETOR AND ROBERT ADAMS EXECUTIVE CHEF

Spinach and Leek Avgolemono Soup

2 Cups sliced leeks
5 Tablespoons butter, divided
1 whole bay leaf
1/2 Cup diced carrots
1/2 teaspoon finely diced lemon zest
1/2 Cup white wine
2 quarts chicken stock
Salt and freshly ground black pepper
1/2 pound fresh spinach, coarsely chopped
1/3 Cup finely diced onion
2 egg yolks
3 whole eggs
1/2 Cup lemon juice

Melt 4 tablespoons butter in a 4-quart saucepan, and add leeks, carrots and bay leaf. Cook over medium-low heat until tender. Add wine, chicken stock and lemon zest, and simmer for 20 minutes. Season with salt and pepper.

Sauté onions in 1 tablespoon butter for 4 to 5 minutes or until onions are barely translucent. Add spinach, and cook until barely wilted. Add spinach mixture to the broth.

In a large bowl whisk egg yolks and whole eggs with lemon juice. Temper by adding 1 cup hot broth while whisking vigorously. Slowly add egg and lemon mixture to hot broth. Do not boil. Continue to cook over low heat until soup is slightly thickened and creamy. Serve hot or cold.

Portobello Mushrooms with Fresh Tomato and Manouri Cheese

6 medium-size portobello mushroom caps, stems removed
2 Tablespoons pure olive oil
1/3 Cup lemon juice
Salt and freshly ground black pepper
6 sprigs fresh thyme
12 slices fresh tomato (1/4-inches thick)
6 slices Manouri cheese (1/4-inches thick) [See *Editor's Note*]
2 Tablespoons extra virgin olive oil
2 Tablespoons balsamic vinegar
10 basil leaves, coarsely chopped

Toss mushroom caps with olive oil, thyme, salt and pepper. Grill or roast mushrooms 7 to 8 minutes per side. Remove from heat, toss with lemon juice, and set aside.

Season tomato slices with salt, pepper and basil. Set aside. Sprinkle pepper liberally over Manouri cheese slices. Place on parchment paper, and roast in 350°F oven for 3 minutes.

To Assemble

Place 1 mushroom, gill side up on each plate, top with tomato slice, then Manouri cheese, and sprinkle all with basil. Combine olive oil and balsamic vinegar, and drizzle over top. Serve immediately.

Grilled Lamb with Eggplant and Roasted Onion-Red Pepper Relish

        2 pounds boneless lamb leg
            cut into 3/4-inch medallions
        1 Cup olive oil
        6 cloves garlic, sliced
        1/4 Cup coarsely chopped fresh oregano
        Salt and freshly ground black pepper
        2 sticks canela [See *Editor's Note*]

Combine oil, garlic and herbs, and mix well. Pour over lamb medallions, and marinate for 2 hours in refrigerator.

For the Relish

        2 medium-size eggplants
        2 roasted red bell peppers
        2 roasted onions
        1 pound fresh spinach, washed,
            stems removed
        1 Cup olive oil, divided
        1/3 Cup lemon juice
        1 Tablespoon red wine vinegar
        1 clove garlic, coarsely chopped

Using a vegetable peeler make alternating vertical stripes around eggplant, removing and discarding 1/4-inch strips of skin. Slice eggplant into 1/2-inch slices, sprinkle slices with salt, and drain in colander for 20 minutes. Pat slices dry with paper towels. Brush each slice with olive oil, and grill until golden brown, about 4 to 5 minutes per side.

Place 2 large yellow onions, unpeeled, and 2 whole red bell peppers in a 350°F oven for 30 to 45 minutes or until onions are tender and skin on peppers has turned black. Remove onions from oven, and cut into large chunks. Place peppers in a paper bag for about 10 minutes. Remove peppers from bag, and peel and seed them. Cut peppers into 2-inch strips.

Heat a sauté pan until hot. Add 1 tablespoon olive oil and spinach. Cook until spinach is barely wilted. Remove pan from heat, and reserve.

In a large bowl combine remaining olive oil, lemon juice, red wine vinegar and garlic. Add wilted spinach, roasted peppers and onions, and toss to combine. Set aside.

Remove lamb from marinade, and grill over medium-high heat for 10 to 15 minutes or until medium-rare.

To Assemble

Place 1 slice grilled eggplant in center of each plate. Top eggplant with a spoonful of onion-pepper-spinach mixture. Top with grilled lamb. Garnish with strip of grilled red pepper, and spoon juice from relish over presentation. Serve immediately.

Grilled Lobster Salad with Citrus Vinaigrette

        2 live lobsters (1 1/4 pounds each)

For the Court Bouillon

        2 Cups white wine
        2 Cups diced onion
        2 Cups freshly squeezed orange juice
        1 Tablespoon minced fresh ginger
        4 Cups water

Mix all ingredients, and bring to a boil. Add lobsters, cover, and cook for 6 minutes. Remove lobsters from liquid, and cool. Carefully remove meat from tail and claws so that meat is kept in whole pieces.

For the Vinaigrette

        1 inch fresh ginger root, peeled and minced
        3 Tablespoons minced shallots
        1 1/2 Cups freshly squeezed orange juice
        1 Tablespoon champagne vinegar
        2/3 Cup olive oil
        2 teaspoons fresh lemon juice
        Salt and freshly ground black pepper

Using small mixing bowl and wire whisk, combine ginger, shallots, orange juice and vinegar. While whisking vigorously add olive oil in a slow, steady stream. Add lemon juice, salt and pepper. Taste, and adjust seasonings if necessary. Reserve.

To Assemble the Salad

        Lobster meat
        Salt and freshly ground black pepper
        2 Tablespoons olive oil
        1 Cup peeled, seeded and diced cucumber
        1 Cup seeded and diced red bell pepper
        12 ounces mixed baby greens
        2 oranges, peeled and sectioned

Cut lobster tail meat in half vertically. Season with olive oil, salt and pepper. Grill over hot charcoal fire or on a ribbed cast iron griddle until grill marks are medium-brown, about 4 minutes. Remove from grill, and slice into 1/4-inch thick slices.

In large metal mixing bowl toss greens, sliced lobster, shelled claw meat, cucumber and bell pepper together with vinaigrette. Arrange on plates, and garnish with orange sections.

▼▼▼▼▼▼▼▼▼▼▼▼▼▼▼▼▼▼▼▼▼▼▼▼▼▼▼▼▼▼▼
Banana Rum Napoleon

For the Pastry Cream
> 2 Cups half-and-half, divided
> 1/2 Cup heavy cream
> 3/4 Cup sugar
> 1/4 Cup cornstarch
> 6 egg yolks
> 1/2 Cup banana puree
> 2 Tablespoons Myers's® dark rum

Heat 1 1/2 cups half-and-half with sugar, and bring to a boil. Combine cornstarch with remaining 1/2 cup of cream, and whisk until incorporated. Add egg yolks to cornstarch mixture. Whisk 1/2 cup hot cream and sugar mixture into egg yolks to temper them. While stirring constantly pour warm yolk mixture back into hot cream. Cook over medium-high heat until mixture bubbles. Whisk vigorously for 2 minutes. Remove from heat, transfer to a clean bowl, and cool.

Beat heavy cream until soft peaks form. In a separate bowl whisk cooled cream and egg mixture with pureed banana, and fold in whipped cream and rum.

For the Phyllo Pastry
> 6 sheets phyllo dough, thawed
>   [See *Cook's Notes & Glossary*]
> 8 Tablespoons (1 stick) butter, melted
> 1 Cup sugar
> 1 teaspoon ground cinnamon
> 1/2 Cup chopped walnuts

Brush a baking sheet with melted butter and place 2 layers of phyllo onto sheet. Mix sugar and cinnamon, and sprinkle one third of mixture evenly over pastry. Top with 2 more layers phyllo, brush with butter, and sprinkle another third cinnamon-sugar mixture over pastry. Repeat process until there are 6 layers of dough. Cover top layer of phyllo with melted butter, cinnamon-sugar and walnuts. Using a sharp knife, cut into 18 equal portions. Cook in a 400°F oven for 15 minutes or until browned.

To Assemble
> 2 ripe bananas, peeled and sliced

Place 1 phyllo square on each plate. Spoon a dollop of pastry cream on top, and arrange 2 to 3 slices of banana in the cream. Top with another dollop of cream and a second layer of phyllo. Continue until 3 layers of pastry are used. End with phyllo, and dust with powdered sugar. Serve immediately.

Editor's Notes
• *Manouri cheese is a Greek cheese available at Wellspring and other area gourmet stores. It is a firm, white cheese made from sheep's milk.*
• *Canela is also called true cinnamon or Ceylon cinnamon. It looks like what we know as stick cinnamon, but is soft and flaky. The flavor is also softer and not as strong as cinnamon. Canela is available at Wellspring and other area specialty stores.*

Sea Bass with Two Black Bean Sauces

MICHAEL PALOMBO
EXECUTIVE CHEF

Carolina Inn's Carolina Crossroads Restaurant & Bar

Located in the historic Carolina Inn in Chapel Hill, Carolina Crossroads is a product of the inn's recent multi-million dollar renovation. Chef Michael Palombo draws from an extensive repertoire of innovative recipes including a few from his mother— as in the case of Struvallers, the traditional Italian sweet served with coffee and dessert during the Christmas holidays.

▼▼▼▼▼▼▼▼▼▼▼▼▼▼▼▼▼▼▼▼▼▼▼▼▼▼▼▼▼▼
Butternut Squash Soup

   3 Cups fresh-baked butternut squash
      (approximately 1 large squash)
      [See *Editor's Note*]
   2 Cups coarsely chopped yellow onions
   2 Tablespoons butter
   6 Cups vegetable or chicken stock
   1 Tablespoon curry powder
   3 Tablespoons honey
   1/4 Cup dry sherry
   3/4 Cup heavy cream
   1 Tablespoon salt
   1/2 teaspoon freshly ground black pepper

For the Garnish
   2 Tablespoons pumpkin seeds,
      roasted and salted
   3 Tablespoons chopped fresh chives
   1/2 Cup heavy cream, whipped until
      slightly thickened

Cut squash in half and remove seeds. Place cut side down on a baking sheet, and bake at 350°F for 1 hour or until soft. Scoop out the flesh, and puree in a food processor or blender.

Sauté onions in butter until soft, then puree in blender. In a soup pot combine pureed onions, squash and stock. Bring to a simmer. Add curry powder, honey and sherry. Simmer for 10 minutes. Strain through a fine-mesh strainer, and return to a clean soup pot. Add cream, salt and pepper.

Garnish with toasted pumpkin seeds and chopped fresh chives. Drizzle with cream and serve.

▼▼▼▼▼▼▼▼▼▼▼▼▼▼▼▼▼▼▼▼▼▼▼▼▼▼▼▼▼▼
Black-Cherry-Smoked Pork Tenderloin with Beet Vinaigrette and Chive Oil

For the Pork Tenderloin
   2 pork tenderloins
   1 pound black cherry wood chips
      (or apple, pecan or hickory chips)
   4 Cups mesclun or mixed greens

Clean tenderloins of all fat and sinews. Smoke in a home smoker or grill for approximately 15 minutes. Refrigerate until chilled.

For the Beet Vinaigrette
>8 ounces whole fresh beets
>1/2 Cup white balsamic vinegar
>1 1/2 Cups peanut oil
>1/4 Cup water
>2 Tablespoons minced shallots
>1 teaspoon minced garlic
>Salt and freshly ground black pepper

Place whole beets on a baking sheet, and roast in a 350°F oven for 45 minutes to 1 hour or until soft when pierced with a fork. Remove from oven. Let cool. Trim ends off beets, and slip peel off, and discard. Place peeled beets in blender, and add water, vinegar, shallots and garlic. Blend until pureed. While blender is running, add oil in a slow, steady stream. Blend until smooth and thickened. Salt and pepper to taste. Reserve.

For the Chive Oil
>1/2 Cup plus 2 Tablespoons chopped chives
>1 Cup extra virgin olive oil

Place 1/2 cup chives in blender with oil. Blend until smooth and well combined. Transfer to a saucepan, and simmer over low heat for 30 minutes. Remove from heat, and let cool. Strain through a fine-mesh strainer. Chop remaining chives, and add to the oil.

To Assemble
>Carve pork into thin slices, and arrange over mixed greens. Drizzle with beet vinaigrette, and garnish with chive oil.

▼▼▼▼▼▼▼▼▼▼▼▼▼▼▼▼▼▼▼▼▼▼▼▼▼▼▼▼
Sea Bass with Two Black Bean Sauces

For the Black Bean Ginger Sauce
>1 1/2 Cups cooked black beans
>1/4 Cup soy sauce
>1/2 Cup teriyaki sauce
>1/2 Cup chicken stock
>2 1/2 Tablespoons minced fresh ginger
>1 Cup sugar
>1 1/2 teaspoons minced garlic
>2 Tablespoons cornstarch
>   dissolved in 3 Tablespoons cold water

Put soy sauce, teriyaki sauce, stock, ginger, sugar and garlic into a stock pot. Bring to a boil and slowly add dissolved cornstarch. Boil, stirring constantly, until a syrupy consistency is achieved. Add black beans, and stir to combine.

For the Creamy Black Bean Sauce
>1 Cup cooked black beans
>1/2 Cup chicken stock
>1/2 Cup heavy cream
>1/2 teaspoon ground cumin
>2 Tablespoons butter

Puree beans and chicken stock in blender. Add cream, and transfer to a saucepan. Simmer for 15 minutes. Add cumin, butter, salt and pepper. Reserve.

For the Polenta
>1 Cup quick-cooking polenta
>Salt and freshly ground black pepper
>1 Tablespoon chopped mixed herbs,
>   such as chives, basil and parsley
>1 teaspoon minced garlic
>2 Tablespoons minced chives
>3 Tablespoons olive oil, divided
>3 ounces Montrechet-type goat cheese

Cook polenta according to package instructions. In a small skillet sauté garlic, chives and fresh herbs in 1 tablespoon olive oil. Add to cooked polenta. Stir in goat cheese until well blended.

Line a loaf pan or mold with plastic wrap. Pour in warm polenta mixture, and cool until set. When cool, remove polenta from mold, and slice into 6 half-inch pieces. Heat 2 tablespoons olive oil in a skillet, and fry polenta slices until crispy and golden.

For the Sautéed Vegetables
>1 red bell pepper, seeded and julienned
>1 yellow bell pepper, seeded and julienned
>Kernels from 2 ears roasted corn
>1/2 Cup snow peas
>2 Tablespoons butter

Sauté vegetables in butter until tender, but not mushy.

For the Crispy Leeks
>2 leeks, white part only
>1/2 Cup all-purpose flour
>Salt and freshly ground black pepper
>Vegetable oil, 2 inches deep in pot or skillet

Clean leeks, and julienne into tiny strips about 2 inches long. Soak leeks in ice water for at least 1 hour. Drain, and wrap in paper towels to fully dry. Put flour, salt and pepper in a plastic bag. Add drained leeks, and shake vigorously to evenly coat each piece. Remove leeks from bag, and shake off excess flour.

Heat vegetable oil to 350°F. Drop a handful of leeks at a time into hot oil. Fry until lightly colored. Remove with a slotted spoon, and drain on paper towels.

For the Chilean Sea Bass
> 6 Chilean sea bass fillets (6-ounces each),
>   skinned and boned
> 2 Tablespoons peanut oil

Heat grill pan or cast iron skillet until very hot. Add peanut oil. When hot add fish fillets, and cook until crispy. Carefully turn fillets over, and brown other side.

To Assemble

Place 1 spoonful of Creamy Black Bean Sauce on the right-hand side of each plate. Spread to cover half the plate. Place 1 spoonful of Black Bean Ginger sauce on other half, and spread to cover remainder of plate. Place 1 slice fried polenta in center of each plate, and top with sautéed vegetables, then fish fillet, and crown with crispy leeks.

Struvallers
(Honey Balls)

> 3 1/2 Cups all-purpose flour
> 1 Cup sugar
> 3 eggs
> 8 Tablespoons (1 stick) butter
> 1 teaspoon vanilla extract
> 1 teaspoon baking powder
> 1 1/2 Cups honey
> Oil for frying
> 1/2 Cup chopped candied citrus fruits
> 1 1/2 Cups confetti candy

Sift flour and baking powder together. Set aside. Using an electric mixer combine eggs, vanilla and sugar. Use the dough hook attachment, and add the flour. Knead on medium speed for approximately 10 minutes, or until dough is firm but not sticky. Cover dough with plastic wrap, and refrigerate for 1 hour.

While dough is chilling, combine honey and candied citrus fruits, and set aside. Using your hands, roll a portion of dough into 1-inch balls. Fry dough balls in 350°F oil until golden. Remove from oil, and drain on paper towels. While still warm, roll balls in honey-citrus fruit mixture, and sprinkle all over with confetti candy.

Granny Smith Apple Tart

> 6 tart shells (4-inches wide)
> 5 Granny Smith apples, peeled and cored
> 1/2 Cup sugar
> 1 1/2 teaspoons cinnamon
> Pinch nutmeg
> 6 scoops Cinnamon and Pink Peppercorn
>   Ice Cream (recipe follows)

Slice apples into 1/8-inch thick rings, then cut in half. Toss slices with sugar, cinnamon and nutmeg. Arrange spiced apple slices in unbaked tart shells, and bake at 350°F for 15-20 minutes or until pastry is lightly colored and apples are tender. Remove from oven, and top each tart with crumb topping. Return to oven for 5 to 10 minutes. Serve warm with a scoop of Cinnamon and Pink Peppercorn Ice Cream.

For the Crumb Topping
> 2/3 Cup sugar
> 1/2 Cup all-purpose flour
> 1 teaspoon ground cinnamon
> 4 Tablespoons salted butter
> 1 Cup chopped pecans

Combine all ingredients, and blend until the mixture resembles coarse crumbs.

For the Cinnamon and Pink Peppercorn Ice Cream
> 2 Cups heavy cream
> 1 Cup half-and-half
> 7 egg yolks
> 1 Cup sugar
> 1/2 fresh vanilla bean, cut lengthwise
> 2 teaspoons ground cinnamon
> 1/2 teaspoon pink peppercorns, crushed

Place cream and half-and-half in a saucepan and heat until scalded. Add vanilla bean which has been cut lengthwise to expose the interior. Remove cream from heat, and set aside.

In a mixing bowl placed over hot water, beat sugar and egg yolks until frothy and sugar is dissolved. Remove vanilla bean from cream, and pour egg and sugar mixture into cream. Bring to a simmer while constantly stirring. When cream is slightly thickened remove from heat, and cool. Add cinnamon and crushed pink peppercorns. Freeze in ice cream machine according to manufacturer's directions.

Editor's Note
• *Butternut squash was out of season when this recipe was tested. We used a Red Kuri squash with superb results. This soup is also delicious cold, garnished with chopped chives.*

Rigatoni alla Vodka

CLAUDE ROSSINI
CHEF-PROPRIETOR

Claudio's in Raleigh owes its provenance

to chef-owner Claude Rossini's devotion to

his native Northern Italian culture. His

restaurant is an upscale, classic trattoria

where the locals go for robust flavors,

friendly conversation and good times.

▼▼▼▼▼▼▼▼▼▼▼▼▼▼▼▼▼▼▼▼▼▼▼▼▼▼▼▼
Pasta e Fagioli
(Bean and Pasta Soup)

1 1/2 pounds dried great Northern or
    cannellini beans
Unsalted chicken stock or water
    to cover beans by 2 inches
1 pound prosciutto skin or rind
    [See *Editor's Note*]
1 1/4 Cups chopped yellow onion
1 1/2 pounds canned whole tomatoes
1/2 teaspoon white pepper
1 Tablespoon garlic powder
2 Knorr® brand chicken bouillon cubes
Salt to taste
1/4 pound tubetti pasta cooked in salted
    water until tender, drained and reserved.

Place beans in a deep heavy pot, and cover with stock and/or water by 2 inches. Bring to a rolling boil, and cook for 45 minutes to 1 hour. Check frequently, and keep covered with stock or water by 1 inch.

Put prosciutto skins in a roasting pan, and bake at 450°F for 30 to 45 minutes or until skins becomes dark brown and crispy, and oil is rendered. Strain oil into saucepan, and allow to cool slightly. Place saucepan over medium heat, and add chopped onion. Sauté until onions are translucent, then add tomatoes, and simmer about 30 minutes. Add tomato mixture to beans along with white pepper and garlic powder. Cook until beans are nearly done. Add chicken bouillon cubes, and cook for 10 minutes more.

Place a heaping tablespoon of cooked pasta in a bowl, and ladle soup over it.

To turn this soup into a meal of its own add diced grilled chicken or cooked sausage.

Eggplant Toscanna

For the Eggplant
> 1 to 2 large eggplants, sliced into 18
>   1/2-inch diagonal slices
> 1/2 Cup olive oil
> 1 Tablespoon minced garlic
> 1/4 teaspoon salt
> 1/2 teaspoon freshly ground black pepper
> 1 Tablespoon chopped fresh basil

Combine oil, garlic, herbs and spices. Brush each slice of eggplant on both sides with oil mixture. Grill eggplant over very hot coals until grill marks appear. Eggplant should be tender but not soft.

For the Marinara Sauce
> 1/4 Cup olive oil
> 1 Tablespoon sliced fresh garlic
> 2 cans (1 pound 12 ounces each)
>   whole Italian-style tomatoes
> 1 teaspoon garlic powder
> 6 fresh basil leaves, shredded
> 1 teaspoon dried basil
> 1 teaspoon dried Greek oregano
> Salt and ground white pepper to taste
> 1 teaspoon sugar
>   (if sauce is too tart for your taste)

In a large skillet over medium-high heat sauté garlic until golden. Be careful not to let it get too dark or it will taste bitter. Add tomatoes, salt and pepper. Add garlic powder and herbs. Simmer 30 to 40 minutes stirring occasionally to break up tomatoes, but do not make sauce smooth.

To Assemble
> 1 pound fresh mozzarella cheese
> 3 red or yellow bell peppers, roasted,
>   peeled and seeded
> 12 slices fresh tomato (1/4-inches thick)

In 6 individual baking dishes layer 1 slice of tomato, 1 slice of eggplant, 1 slice of mozzarella, then 1 slice of roasted pepper. Repeat layering process ending with eggplant. Do not add oil. Place baking dishes in a 450°F oven for 5 minutes to melt cheese and warm other ingredients.

Place a spoonful of marinara sauce in center of each plate. Top with layered eggplant, and garnish with fresh basil.

Rigatoni alla Vodka

> 1 1/2 pounds rigatoni pasta
> 6 Tablespoons salted butter
> 3 teaspoons chopped shallots
> 2 1/2 Cups sliced shiitake mushrooms
> 1 1/4 Cups sun-dried tomatoes, julienned
> 2 1/2 Cups Fresh Tomato Sauce
>   (recipe below)
> 3 ounces vodka
> 2 1/2 Cups heavy cream
> 1 1/4 Cups half-and-half
> 3/4 teaspoon white pepper
> 3/4 teaspoon garlic powder
> 1/2 teaspoon salt
> 2 1/2 Cups early peas, cooked without salt

Cook rigatoni according to package instructions. Reserve.

Melt butter in a large skillet over medium-high heat. When foam has subsided add shallots, and cook until translucent. Add mushrooms and sun-dried tomatoes. Sauté until mushrooms are soft. Deglaze pan with vodka.

Add Fresh Tomato Sauce, heavy cream, half-and-half, pepper, garlic powder and salt. Cook over medium heat stirring occasionally until sauce thickens and reduces slightly. Add peas, stir gently, and pour over cooked rigatoni.

For the Fresh Tomato Sauce
> 6 large ripe tomatoes
> 1/4 Cup olive oil
> 3 teaspoons minced fresh garlic
> 1/8 teaspoon salt
> 1/8 teaspoon freshly ground black pepper

Core tomatoes, and blanch in boiling water for 2 minutes. Remove, drain and rinse under cold running water. Drain well. Remove peel and crush tomatoes with your hands. Place in a large saucepan.

In a small skillet, sauté garlic in olive oil until light brown. Strain. Discard garlic, and add oil to tomatoes. Cook over low heat for approximately 1 hour or until reduced by half. Season with salt and pepper. Makes about 2 1/2 cups.

Chicken Breast Stuffed with Wild Rice and Spinach

For the Stuffing

> 1 Cup cooked wild rice
> 1 Tablespoon clarified butter
> 1/4 Cup sliced shiitake mushrooms
> 1/2 Cup chopped fresh spinach
> 1 Tablespoon crushed pine nuts

Sauté mushrooms, spinach and pine nuts in butter and combine with rice. Set aside.

For the Chicken and the Sauce

> 6 boneless chicken breasts (8-ounces each),
>   butterflied, skin intact
> Olive oil for sautéing
> 3 Tablespoons butter
> 3 Tablespoons chopped shallots
> 3 Tablespoons Madeira wine
> 3 Cups prepared beef or veal brown sauce
>   [See *Editor's Note*]
> Salt and freshly ground black pepper
> 1/4 teaspoon garlic powder
> 1/2 teaspoon chopped fresh sage leaves

Pound each chicken breast to equal thickness. Put 1/2 cup of stuffing in center of each breast. Fold sides of chicken inward so that they envelop the stuffing. Roll chicken from top to bottom, and set aside.

Sauté shallots in butter until transparent. Add Madeira and brown sauce, and reduce by half. Flavor sauce with garlic powder, sage, salt and pepper. Set aside, and keep warm.

Heat olive oil in a heavy skillet. When oil is hot add stuffed chicken breasts, seam-side down. The heat will immediately seal in the stuffing. Allow to cook for about 3 minutes and turn to brown other side. Remove chicken from skillet. Place 1 breast on each plate. Slice as you would a loaf of bread, but not all the way through. Separate segments just enough to expose stuffing. Strain sauce over each breast, and serve immediately.

Tiramisù

> 8 eggs, separated
> 1 Cup sugar, divided
> 1 1/2 teaspoons sweet Marsala wine
> 1 Tablespoon vanilla extract
> 16 ounces mascarpone cheese
> 2 dozen ladyfingers
> 2 Cups strong espresso
> 1 Tablespoon Triple Sec
> Unsweetened cocoa powder for dusting

In a mixing bowl add 1/2 cup sugar to egg yolks, Marsala and vanilla. Beat until frothy and pale yellow. Beat in mascarpone cheese. Refrigerate.

Beat egg whites to soft peaks, add remaining sugar, and beat until soft peaks reform. Carefully fold whites into yolk mixture.

Blend espresso and Triple Sec. Dip each ladyfinger into the mixture. Layer bottom of a 9-by 13-inch casserole with ladyfingers. Cover with half the cheese and custard mixture. Add another layer of ladyfingers, then top with remaining cheese and egg custard. Sprinkle top layer of custard with cocoa, and chill thoroughly.
Serves 12.

Editor's Note

• *If you cannot find prosciutto skin or pancetta you can substitute 3 tablespoons renderings from side meat seasoned with 1/2 teaspoon nutmeg, 1 teaspoon brown sugar and 1 large pinch of cloves. In this case reduce the bouillon cube to one.*

• *Prepared beef or veal brown sauce can be purchased at area gourmet markets or you can make your own by reducing homemade, unsalted, veal or beef stock until it thickens and turns into a syrup.*

Baked Goat Cheese and Black-Eyed Pea Salad

CORY MATTSON
EXECUTIVE CHEF

Award-winning and nationally acclaimed, the Fearrington House in Fearrington Village is under the stewardship of chef Cory Mattson. When asked about his cuisine, chef Mattson was quoted in Bon Appétit *magazine; "Take the authentic flavors of this mid-Atlantic region...I think of them as my toys in the sandbox. Then add my classical training and my personal interests and style—I'm absolutely in love with northern Italian, Asian and southern American cooking—and you end up with my menu."*

Fruit Gazpacho

2 Tablespoons olive oil
3/4 Cup chopped shallots
1 teaspoon chopped garlic
1/2 Cup chopped leek, white part only
1 red bell pepper, seeded and
    coarsely chopped
1 yellow bell pepper, seeded and
    coarsely chopped
1 green bell pepper, seeded and
    coarsely chopped
1 European cucumber, peeled, seeded
    and chopped
3/4 Cup chopped onion
3 Cups diced cantaloupe
1 1/2 Cups kiwi pulp
1 Cup V-8® juice
1/4 Cup white wine vinegar
2 Tablespoons chopped cilantro leaves
3 Tablespoons fresh lemon juice
3 Tablespoons fresh lime juice
1 Tablespoon salt
2 teaspoons freshly ground black pepper

Heat olive oil in sauté pan over medium-high heat, and add shallots, garlic and leeks. Sauté for 5 minutes. Remove from heat, and cool. Add sautéed vegetables to remaining fruits and vegetables. Place in a blender and blend until completely pureed. Add V-8 juice and citrus juices.

Add salt, pepper and chopped fresh cilantro. Serve chilled.

Salmon Carpaccio

12 salmon medallions (1-ounces each),
  skinned and cleaned
Ask your fishmonger for sushi-quality salmon, and have her/him cut medallions from thickest part of fillet. Make sure salmon is very cold before placing each medallion between 2 sheets of waxed paper and gently pounding until thin. Continue until all medallions are pounded into thin sheets. Refrigerate until ready to use.

For the Onion and Apple Relish
  1 Cup diced red onions
  1 Cup diced Granny Smith apples
  1 Cup peeled, seeded and diced tomatoes
  1/4 Cup finely minced fresh basil
Combine ingredients, and set aside.

For the Dressing
  1/3 Cup B&B® liqueur
  1/2 Cup extra virgin olive oil
  1/2 Cup white balsamic vinegar
  Salt and freshly ground black pepper
Pour B&B into small skillet, and heat over medium heat until warm. Turn off heat, and use a long wooden match to carefully flame B&B. Tilt pan slightly until flames die out. Pour B&B into bowl with olive oil and vinegar, and whisk until combined. Add salt and pepper to taste.

To Assemble
  Arrange 2 slices salmon on each plate, and top with relish and dressing. Serve immediately.

Baked Goat Cheese and Black-Eyed Pea Salad

For the Baked Goat Cheese
  1 pound fresh goat cheese log
  2 Cups extra virgin olive oil
  3 Tablespoons mixed, chopped fresh herbs,
    such as rosemary, thyme, basil and sage
  1 Cup fresh breadcrumbs
Cut goat cheese log into 3/4-inch thick slices. Mix oil and chopped herbs, and pour over cheese. Marinate at least 6 hours. Just before use remove cheese from oil, and coat with fresh breadcrumbs on all sides. Set aside. Reserve oil marinade.

For the Black-Eyed Pea Salad
  1 pound black-eyed peas
  2 cloves garlic, peeled
  1 small onion, peeled and quartered
  2 bay leaves
  1 ham bone
Cover black-eyed peas by 2 inches with cold water. Bring to a boil. Add garlic, onion, bay leaves and ham bone. Cook until tender but not mushy, approximately 40 minutes. Drain, and spread on baking sheet to cool.

For the Apple and Onion Relish
  1 Granny Smith apple, peeled and diced
  3/4 Cup peeled and diced red onion
  1 tomato, peeled, seeded and diced

For the Balsamic Vinaigrette
  1/4 Cup red wine vinegar
  1/4 Cup balsamic vinegar
  Pinch dried thyme
  Pinch dried oregano
  1 teaspoon honey
  1 teaspoon powdered mustard
  1/2 Cup reserved oil marinade
  Salt and freshly ground black pepper
Combine all ingredients except oil in blender, and blend on medium speed until combined. With blender running pour oil in slow, steady stream until mixture is totally combined and thickened. Pour over relish, and combine. Add drained black-eyed peas, mix and set aside.

To Assemble
  1 pound mesclun or mixed baby greens
Bake breaded goat cheese at 350°F for 10 minutes or until lightly colored. Portion greens onto 6 plates. Top each portion of greens with black-eyed pea salad, then with warm goat cheese.

Red Deer Medallions

12 medallions of red deer (3-ounces each),
  seared until medium-rare
  [See *Editor's Note*]
4 Tablespoons minced shallots
1 teaspoon crushed garlic
1 teaspoon clarified butter
1 Tablespoon fresh thyme
1 Tablespoon soy sauce

1/4 Cup B&B liqueur
1/4 Cup red wine
1/4 Cup heavy cream
1 teaspoon butter, softened

In medium-size skillet combine shallots, garlic, clarified butter and thyme. Heat over medium heat for 2 minutes. Add remaining ingredients except 1 teaspoon butter, and cook over medium-high heat until liquid reduces by one third. Swirl in butter, strain and serve over medallions.

Pear and Fig Tart with B&B Ice Cream and Caramel Sauce

For the Tart Shells
  15 sheets phyllo dough, thawed
    [See *Cook's Notes & Glossary*]
  8 Tablespoons (1 stick) butter, melted
  Powdered (10X) sugar

Cut phyllo sheets into 6-inch squares. Use 5 squares per tart. Brush each square with butter, and sprinkle with powdered sugar. Stack 5 squares, rotating each square to form a star pattern. Press stacked phyllo into 6 individual tart pans or muffin cups. Bake in a 350°F oven for 5 minutes or until lightly colored. Remove from oven, and reserve.

For the Filling
  1/3 Cup blanched almonds
  6 1/2 Tablespoons powdered (10X) sugar
  6 Tablespoons butter
  3 egg whites
  4 Tablespoons all-purpose flour
  1 teaspoon vanilla extract
  1/4 Cup sugar
  1/8 teaspoon salt
  2 pears, peeled, cored and diced
  2 ripe figs, sliced horizontally

Use food processor to grind almonds and powdered sugar together. Reserve.

Melt butter in small sauté pan, and cook until golden. Remove from heat, and set aside. Combine egg whites, flour, almond-powdered sugar mixture, vanilla, sugar and salt in bowl of electric mixer. Beat until smooth, about 2 minutes. Add brown butter, and beat until incorporated. Divide filling among pre-baked tart shells. Top with diced pears and sliced figs. Bake in a 350°F oven for approximately 15 minutes.

For the B&B Ice Cream
  1 quart heavy cream
  2 Cups milk
  1 vanilla bean, split lengthwise
  12 egg yolks
  1 1/2 Cups sugar
  1/2 Cup B&B liqueur

In a saucepan bring cream, milk and vanilla bean to a boil. Remove from heat. Whisk egg yolks and sugar until well combined. Then whisking constantly pour half of hot cream into egg mixture. Return all to remaining cream in saucepan. Place over medium heat, and stir constantly until mixture thickly coats the back of a spoon. Do not boil. Remove from heat, strain and chill. Add B&B, and freeze in ice cream machine according to manufacturer's instructions.

For the Caramel Sauce
  3/4 Cups sugar
  1/2 Cup corn syrup
  1 Cup cream
  4 Tablespoons butter

Bring sugar and corn syrup to boil in a heavy saucepan. Continue to boil until mixture turns the color of tea. Carefully add cream, and return to boil. Remove from heat, and add butter. Reserve.

To Assemble
  Place a large spoonful of caramel sauce in the middle of each plate. Place a warm tart in center of sauce, and top with scoop of ice cream. Drizzle with additional caramel sauce, and serve immediately.

Editor's Note
• *Filet mignon can be substituted for red deer. Red deer can be ordered from D'Artagnan — 1-800-327-8246 (1-800-DARTAGNAN).*

Moroccan Lamb and Lentil Soup

Shrimp, Mushroom and Spinach Timbale with Red Pepper Coulis

Israeli Couscous Risotto with Shrimp, Asparagus, Carrots and Snow Peas

MO ZAIDEN
CHEF DE CUISINE

The Fearrington Market Cafe is located in the Village of Fearrington in Pittsboro. The cafe, situated above the market, is light and airy, and sports an enticing international menu for both lunch and dinner. The market carries specialty foods and charming gifts and household accessories.

Moroccan Lamb and Lentil Soup

1 Tablespoon olive oil
2 Tablespoons chopped garlic
1 Cup chopped onion
1 pound lamb, trimmed and cut into cubes
1 Cup dried lentils
3/4 Cup diced carrots
1/2 Cup diced celery rib
3/4 Cup diced green bell pepper
2 pounds tomatoes, peeled, seeded
    and chopped
1 teaspoon tumeric
Pinch saffron
1 teaspoon ground cinnamon
1/4 teaspoon ground ginger
2 quarts water
1/4 Cup chopped parsley
1/4 Cup chopped cilantro leaves
Lemon wedges for garnish

Heat oil in a large soup pot. Add garlic, onion and lamb, and sauté for 3 minutes. Add vegetables, dry spices and lentils, and stir to coat. Add water, and simmer for up to 90 minutes. Midway through the cooking add salt and pepper. Ten minutes before serving add cilantro and parsley. Ladle into bowls, and garnish with lemon wedges.

Shrimp, Mushroom and Spinach Timbale with Red Pepper Coulis

2 eggs
1 Cup heavy cream
1 Tablespoon butter
1 pound fresh spinach
2 Tablespoons olive oil
1 teaspoon minced garlic
18 shrimp, peeled and deveined,
    split horizontally
2 1/4 Cups julienned shiitake mushrooms

Using a wire whisk combine eggs and cream, and set aside.

In a large skillet over medium heat melt butter. When foam has subsided add fresh spinach, and cook until wilted. Push spinach to the side while tilting the pan and pressing spinach to release as much liquid as possible. Pour off, and discard liquid.

Using 5 layers of super-absorbent paper towels place spinach on towels and roll up, pressing to release all moisture. Repeat as many times as necessary to remove moisture from spinach.

Heat a large skillet over high heat. When hot add olive oil. Add minced garlic, and sauté for 30 seconds. Add mushrooms, and toss to combine. Cook for 2 to 3 minutes or until tender. Add shrimp, and toss until first pink color appears. Remove pan from heat.

Butter 6 6-ounce timbale molds. Place a portion of spinach in bottom of each mold, about 1/8 inch deep. Place shrimp on top of spinach to come half way up the side of each mold. Top shrimp with mushrooms.

Using a ladle spoon in egg and cream mixture until each mold is filled. Tap molds against solid surface to ensure that liquid is distributed evenly. Don't tip the timbales as you don't want liquid to seep under the spinach.

Place timbales in a baking pan, and pour boiling water into pan, being careful not to splash any water into timbales. Water should come half way up sides of molds. Bake in a 350°F oven for 30 minutes or until filling is browned on top. Remove from water bath, and let timbales cool for 5 to 10 minutes before unmolding. Timbales can rest on top of stove for up to 1 hour before being unmolded.

For the Coulis
1 1/2 Cup diced onion
1 Tablespoon olive oil
2 red bell peppers, peeled, seeded
    and coarsely chopped
1 Cup peeled, seeded
    and coarsely chopped tomato
1/3 Cup white wine
1/3 Cup vegetable or chicken stock

In a skillet sauté onion in olive oil until translucent. Add bell peppers and tomatoes, and sauté for a few more minutes. Add wine and stock, and simmer mixture until it is reduced by two thirds. Put mixture into blender, and blend on high speed for about 30 seconds. Pass through a fine-mesh strainer, and reserve.

To Assemble and Serve
Heat coulis, and put a generous spoonful in the middle of each plate. Unmold each timbale, and place in center of sauce, spinach side up.

Israeli Couscous Risotto with Shrimp, Asparagus, Carrots and Snow Peas

Boiling water and salt for blanching
2 medium-size carrots, thinly julienned
1/2 pound fresh asparagus, cut into
    1-inch lengths
1/2 Cup frozen or fresh green peas
4 ounces snow peas, trimmed,
    cut diagonally in half
1 red bell pepper, seeded and julienned
4 Tablespoons olive oil
1/4 Cup minced shallots
1 package (10-ounces) couscous
1/4 Cup white wine
2 1/2 Cups chicken stock
24 shrimp, peeled and deveined
1 Tablespoon minced fresh garlic
2 Tablespoons butter
1/4 Cup grated Parmesan cheese
2 Tablespoons finely chopped Italian parsley
Salt and freshly ground black pepper

Bring pot of water to a boil, then add 1 tablespoon salt for every 3 quarts water. Add carrots to boiling water, and cook for 3 minutes. Add asparagus, peas and snow peas, and cook for 2 minutes, then add bell pepper and cook for 1 minute. Using a slotted spoon, transfer vegetables to bowl filled with ice water. Strain, and keep vegetables refrigerated until needed.

Bring stock to a boil and keep warm.

Heat a large saucepan over moderate heat. When hot add 2 tablespoons olive oil. Add shallots, and cook for 4 minutes. Add couscous, and stir to coat. Add wine, and simmer until evaporated, about 2 to 3 minutes. Add stock, and stir. Remove pan from heat, cover and let sit. The couscous is done when tender but still slightly chewy—about 5 minutes.

Heat another pan over high heat, and add remaining 2 tablespoons olive oil. When hot add shrimp, and sauté until pink, about 1 minute. Add vegetables, salt, pepper and garlic. Toss for 1 minute. Add couscous to the vegetables, and stir. Remove pan from heat, and add butter, Parmesan cheese and parsley. Toss together, and serve.

▼▼▼▼▼▼▼▼▼▼▼▼▼▼▼▼▼▼▼▼▼▼▼▼▼▼▼▼

Kelly's Tiramisù

    2 Cups dark coffee
    1 1/2 Tablespoons instant espresso powder
    1/4 Cup dark brown sugar
    1 teaspoon brandy
    1 pound mascarpone cheese
    1 Cup sugar, divided
    1/3 vanilla bean, split lengthwise,
        pulp reserved
    Pinch of salt
    2 Tablespoons dark rum, such as Myers's®
    1 1/4 Cups heavy cream

Combine coffee, instant espresso, brown sugar and brandy. Set aside. Using an electric mixer blend cheese, 1/2 cup sugar, vanilla bean pulp and salt. Be careful not to overmix. Stir in rum, and set aside. In a separate bowl whip heavy cream and remaining 1/2 cup sugar together until stiff peaks form. Add cheese mixture and gently combine. Set aside.

For the Hot Milk Sponge Cake
    1/3 Cup milk
    3 1/2 Tablespoons butter
    5 egg yolks
    5 whole eggs
    1 1/4 Cups sugar
    2 teaspoons vanilla extract
        (or flavoring of your choice)
    1 1/4 Cups cake flour (See *Editor's Note*)
    1 teaspoon baking powder

In a saucepan over medium heat warm butter and milk. When butter has completely melted set pan aside to cool. Whip egg yolks, whole eggs and sugar until mixture is tripled in volume. Add flavoring, and incorporate. Sift flour together with baking powder, and gently fold into egg mixture. Add milk, and blend gently so as not to lose volume.

Line a 12- by 17-inch baking pan (with sides) with parchment paper. Or use 2 smaller baking pans. Grease parchment paper. Pour mixture into baking pan(s), and bake at 375°F for 15 to 20 minutes or until cake is lightly browned and cooked through. Cool.

To Assemble
    3 Tablespoons unsweetened cocoa powder
Soak sponge cake with cooled coffee mixture. Using a glass bowl or loaf pan start with a layer of soaked sponge cake, then add a layer of cheese mixture. Sprinkle cheese mixture with cocoa and repeat layering process. End with a layer of cheese mixture and a heavy sprinkling of cocoa powder. Chill.

Editor's Note
• *If you cannot find cake flour, sift 2 tablespoons of cornstarch into the bottom of a 1-cup measuring cup. Sift enough all-purpose flour on top of the cornstarch to equal 1 cup. Add an additional 1/4 cup of all-purpose flour to equal the amount called for in this recipe. Pour all of the flour into a bowl and whisk lightly to combine and distribute cornstarch throughout.*

Cioppino (Italian Fish Stew)

A relative newcomer to the restaurant scene in Raleigh, Five Eighteen West is the sister restaurant of Four Eleven West in Chapel Hill. Chef Blaine Nierman presides over the stove where the earthy flavors of Italy are a specialty.

BLAINE NIERMAN
CHEF

▼▼▼▼▼▼▼▼▼▼▼▼▼▼▼▼▼▼▼▼▼▼▼▼▼▼
Tuscan White Bean and Escarole Soup

    8 ounces dried white beans,
        soaked 6 to 8 hours
    1 1/2 Tablespoons olive oil
    2 Cups chopped onion
    1 Cup diced carrots
    2 teaspoons minced garlic
    1 teaspoon dried basil
    1 teaspoon dried thyme
    1 teaspoon dried oregano
    1 whole bay leaf
    2 Cups peeled, seeded and diced tomatoes
    1 1/2 quarts water or chicken stock
    1 1/2 Cups chopped escarole

In a large soup pot over medium-high heat add oil, and sauté onions, carrots and garlic. Add dried herbs and bay leaf, and sauté for 1 minute. Add tomatoes, drained white beans, water or chicken stock, and bring to a boil. Lower heat, and simmer soup until beans are tender and the soup thickens, about 1 to 1 1/2 hours.

Add escarole, and cook until wilted, about 1 minute.

For the Bruschetta
    6 slices sourdough bread (1/2-inches thick)
    1 large garlic clove
    1 Tablespoon extra virgin olive oil
    Extra virgin olive oil for garnish

Rub each slice of bread with garlic clove. Heat oil in a large sauté pan, and sauté bread on both sides until golden brown.

To Assemble
Place 1 piece of bruschetta in a soup bowl, and ladle soup over bread. Drizzle 1 to 2 teaspoons of extra virgin olive oil over top of each serving, and serve immediately.

▼▼▼▼▼▼▼▼▼▼▼▼▼▼▼▼▼▼▼▼▼▼▼▼▼▼
Cornmeal-Crusted Goat Cheese Souffles with Honey-Roasted Hazelnuts and Balsamic Vinaigrette

    2 Tablespoons butter
    2 Tablespoons all-purpose flour
    1/2 Cup milk, scalded
    2 egg yolks
    3 ounces goat cheese, room temperature
    1/2 teaspoon salt, divided
    1/4 teaspoon white pepper
    5 egg whites
    1 teaspoon lemon juice
    Softened butter to line ramekins
    1/4 Cup stone-ground cornmeal
    4 to 5 Cups mixed greens

In a saucepan over moderate heat melt 2 tablespoons butter. When melted whisk in flour. Stir constantly with a wooden spoon for about 5 minutes until mixture turns a blond color, and has a faint nutty aroma. Whisk in scalded milk. Reduce heat to simmer, and cook for 2 minutes. Remove pan from heat, and add egg yolks, goat cheese, 1/4 teaspoon of salt and white pepper. Stir until well blended and goat cheese is melted. Set aside.

Butter 6 ramekins (6-ounces each), and dust each with cornmeal to coat.

Beat egg whites to a soft peak, and add lemon juice and 1/4 teaspoon salt. Continue beating until egg whites are stiff and smooth, but not dry.

Mix one quarter of beaten egg whites into souffle base, then gently fold in remaining whites. Carefully spoon mixture into prepared ramekins. Place ramekins in a shallow pan, and fill with boiling water one quarter way up sides of dishes. Bake in a 400°F oven for 15 minutes. Let cool for 15 minutes, and shake ramekins lightly to loosen. Turn souffles out onto waxed paper.

For the Honey-Roasted Hazelnuts
    2 teaspoons butter
    1/2 Cup hazelnuts
    1/2 Tablespoon honey
    1/2 Tablespoon brown sugar
Heat butter in a skillet. When foam subsides add nuts, honey and sugar, and cook until caramelized, about 5 minutes. Set aside.

For the Balsamic Vinaigrette
    1 teaspoon minced garlic
    1/2 Tablespoon honey
    1 Tablespoon Dijon mustard
    3 Tablespoons water
    2 Tablespoons balsamic vinegar
    1/2 Cup olive oil
    Freshly cracked black pepper
In a bowl combine all ingredients except oil and pepper. Add olive oil in a slow, steady stream while whisking constantly. Season with cracked black pepper.

To Assemble the Salad
Place souffles under a hot broiler for about 1 minute to create a golden crust. Divide mixed greens among 6 salad plates. Place 1 souffle on each portion of greens, and drizzle vinaigrette over the top. Garnish with Honey-Roasted Hazelnuts.

▼▼▼▼▼▼▼▼▼▼▼▼▼▼▼▼▼▼▼▼▼▼▼▼▼▼▼▼

Marinated Salmon over Roasted Garlic Mashed Potatoes with Red Onion Cream Sauce

For the Marinated Salmon
    1/4 Cup olive oil
    1 teaspoon salt
    1/2 teaspoon freshly ground black pepper
    2 teaspoons fresh thyme leaves
    6 salmon fillets (6-ounces each)
Mix oil, salt, pepper and thyme in a non-reactive dish. Add salmon fillets, and marinate in refrigerator for 4 hours.

To cook salmon, use a skillet with an oven-proof handle. Lightly oil bottom of pan, and heat it on top of stove until oil is almost smoking. Place fish skin side down into skillet. Put skillet in a 375°F oven for 10 minutes or until flesh is opaque in center.

For the Roasted Garlic Mashed Potatoes
    1 garlic bulb
    1 1/2 pounds red potatoes
    1/2 Cup milk
    8 Tablespoons (1 stick) butter
Slice stem end off garlic bulb. Drizzle olive oil over cut end of garlic, and wrap in foil. Bake in a 350°F oven for 45 minutes. Remove from oven, and cool, leaving foil-wrap in place.

Place potatoes in a deep pot, and cover with water. Boil and cook until done, about 30 minutes. Drain, and peel.

Heat milk and butter until warm. Unwrap garlic, and squeeze melted garlic cloves out of their skins into milk mixture. Place potatoes in a mixing bowl, and add warm milk and butter. Mash. Keep warm by covering bowl and placing it over (not in) hot water.

For the Red Onion Cream Sauce
    2 Tablespoons olive oil
    2 red onions, thinly sliced
    2 teaspoons minced garlic
    1/2 Cup tawny port
    1/2 Cup dry red wine
    1/2 Cup balsamic vinegar
    1/2 Cup cream
    8 Tablespoons (1 stick) butter
In a skillet over medium heat add olive oil, then add sliced onions. Reduce heat to low, and sauté onions until caramelized, about 15 minutes. Add garlic, and sauté 2 minutes more. Add port, red wine and vinegar, and reduce by half. Reserve.

In a separate skillet over medium-high heat, boil cream until reduced by half. Watch carefully so it doesn't boil over. Stir often with a wooden spoon. When cream is reduced and thickened add it to wine mixture, stir, and cook until thick. Remove from heat, and stir in butter.

Place a scoop of mashed potatoes in center of each plate. Top with baked fish, and spoon red onion sauce over top.

Cioppino
(Italian Fish Stew)

2 Tablespoons olive oil
1/2 Cup chopped onions
2 teaspoons minced garlic
1/2 teaspoon saffron threads
1/2 Cup white wine
3 1/2 Cups fish stock
    (or 1 part bottled clam juice, 1 part water)
3/4 pound medium shrimp, peeled
3/4 pound scallops
1/2 pound salmon fillet
    cut into 3 pieces, 3-inches long
36 mussels
1 1/2 pounds linguine
1 Tablespoon olive oil
2 Tablespoons chopped parsley
2 Tablespoons chopped fresh basil
Salt and freshly ground black pepper

Heat olive oil in a large skillet over medium-high heat. Add onion, and sauté until translucent, then add garlic and saffron. Cook for 1 minute. Add wine and stock, cover, and cook about 6 to 8 minutes. Add seafood, and cook for 2 minutes or until seafood is just barely done.

Cook linguine according to package instructions. Drain pasta, and return it to its cooking pot. Add 1 tablespoon olive oil, and toss to coat pasta. Pour seafood mixture into pot with pasta. Heat quickly over high heat, then add parsley and basil, and season with salt and pepper. Serve in soup plates.

Cranberry Walnut Tart with Caramel Sauce

For the Crust
1 Cup all-purpose flour
1/4 Cup sugar
Pinch salt
1/4 teaspoon baking powder
4 Tablespoons butter
1 egg, beaten

Combine dry ingredients. Use a pastry cutter or 2 knives to incorporate butter into flour mixture until mixture appears crumbly. Use a fork to incorporate egg until dough comes together. Wrap dough in plastic wrap, and chill.

For the Filling
1/4 Cup butter
3 eggs
2/3 Cup brown sugar
2/3 Cup light corn syrup
1/2 teaspoon salt
1 teaspoon vanilla
1 1/4 Cup chopped cranberries
    [See *Editor's Note*]
1 Cup chopped walnuts

Melt butter, then cool. Beat eggs and sugar until well blended. Add melted butter and remaining ingredients, and mix well.

Lightly flour your hands, then press pastry into bottom of a 9-inch springform pan. Place a large piece of parchment paper on top of dough, and add one layer of dried beans to hold down pastry. Bake tart shell for 10 minutes in a 350°F oven. Remove pastry shell from oven, and carefully lift out and discard beans and paper. Allow pastry shell to cool in its springform pan.

Pour filling into pre-cooked tart shell, and return it to oven for about 40 minutes or until filling is set. Remove tart from oven, and allow to cool before removing from springform pan. Slice, and serve with Caramel Sauce.

For the Caramel Sauce
1/2 Cup brown sugar
1 Tablespoon cornstarch
1/4 Cup cold water
1/3 Cup heavy cream
2 Tablespoons light corn syrup
1 Tablespoon butter
1/2 teaspoon vanilla extract

In a heavy saucepan mix sugar and cornstarch. Stir in 1/4 cup cold water, then whisk in cream and corn syrup until smooth. Place pan over high heat, and bring to a boil. Cook for 2 minutes stirring constantly. Remove pan from heat, and stir in butter and vanilla. Serve immediately.

Editor's Note
• *Dried cranberries, available at Hannaford and other area grocery stores, work well if fresh cranberries are not available.*

Greek Pizza For One

TREY CLEVELAND
CHEF

Four Eleven West is a favorite Italian trattoria located on Franklin Street, around the corner from the UNC-Chapel Hill campus. Chef Trey Cleveland is justifiably proud of his wood-fired pizza oven and hardy Italian regional specialties.

Gazpacho

1 Cup peeled, seeded and
    coarsely chopped cucumbers
1/4 Cup seeded and
    coarsely chopped green bell peppers
1/4 Cup coarsely chopped onions
1/4 Cup coarsely chopped yellow squash
1/4 Cup coarsely chopped zucchini
1/2 Cup peeled and
    coarsely chopped carrots
2 teaspoons salt
1/4 teaspoon freshly ground black pepper
1 Tablespoon minced garlic
2 Tablespoons lemon juice
5 Cups tomato juice
1/4 Cup red wine vinegar
1/2 teaspoon ground cumin
2 Tablespoons chopped fresh basil
1/2 Cup olive oil

Add all ingredients except cucumbers and olive oil to blender or food processor, and process in batches. The vegetables should remain chunky, not pureed. Add cucumbers, vinegar and lemon juice and process for 2 seconds, until cucumbers are finely chopped. Combine all batches in a large bowl, add tomato juice and whisk in olive oil.

For the Garnish
> 1/4 Cup peeled, seeded and
> chopped cucumber
> 1/4 Cup peeled, seeded and
> chopped yellow squash
> 1/4 Cup peeled, seeded and
> chopped zucchini
> 1/4 Cup peeled, seeded and
> chopped fresh tomato

Combine and sprinkle on top of soup.

Penne Verdura
(Vegetable Pasta)

For the Roasted Vegetables
> 4 Tablespoons olive oil
> 1 Cup thick julienne cut yellow squash
> 1 Cup thick julienne cut zucchini
> 1 Cup thick julienne cut carrots
> 1 Cup thick julienne cut eggplant
> Salt and freshly ground black pepper

Keeping vegetables separate, coat with olive oil, salt and black pepper to taste. Place on a baking sheet, and roast in a 450°F oven for 10 to 15 minutes or until edges are lightly brown. Let vegetables cool, then combine them, and set aside.

To Complete the Recipe
> 1/4 Cup olive oil
> 4 Cups roasted vegetables (recipe above)
> 2 Cups diced roma tomatoes
> 3/4 Cup white wine
> 1 pound penne pasta, cooked according
> to package instructions
> 2 Tablespoons chopped fresh basil
> 2 Tablespoons chopped fresh oregano
> Chopped fresh parsley for garnish

Heat a large skillet until hot, and add olive oil. Add roasted vegetables and tomatoes, and sauté on high heat for 2 minutes. Add white wine and let mixture cook down until most of the wine has evaporated and sauce is thickened, about 5 minutes. Add cooked pasta and fresh herbs, and cook for 1 to 2 minutes to heat thoroughly. Portion onto plates and sprinkle with fresh parsley.

Oyster Gnocchi with Garlic Butter Sauce

For the Garlic Butter Sauce
> 2 Cups white wine
> 1 Tablespoon minced garlic
> 2 teaspoons salt
> 1/2 teaspoon freshly ground black pepper
> 2 Cups heavy cream
> 1/2 pound butter

In a medium-size saucepan combine wine, garlic, salt and pepper, and reduce by half. Add cream, and cook on medium-high heat until thickened, about 12 minutes. Add butter, and whisk gently to incorporate.

For the Oyster Gnocchi
> 1/2 Cup olive oil
> 18 raw oysters, drained
> 1 Cup semolina flour
> 1/4 Cup diced prosciutto
> 6 Cups cooked gnocchi
> 3/4 Cup sliced arugula leaves
> 3/4 Cup diced roma tomatoes
> 1/4 Cup clam broth
> 1 Cup Garlic Butter Sauce (recipe above)
> Toasted almonds, lemon and
> parsley for garnish

Heat a large skillet until hot. Add oil. Toss oysters in semolina flour, shake off excess and fry until golden on all sides. Remove, drain and hold. Return pan to heat, and add prosciutto and gnocchi, and sauté 1 minute. Be careful not to burn the gnocchi. Add arugula and tomatoes, and sauté for 30 seconds. Deglaze pan with clam broth.

To Assemble
Apportion sautéed vegetables and gnocchi onto 6 plates. Arrange equal amounts of fried oysters on top of vegetables and gnocchi, and drizzle each portion with a spoonful Garlic Butter Sauce. Garnish with toasted almonds, lemon and parsley. Serve immediately.

Greek Pizza For One

1 Tablespoon garlic oil
1/4 Cup grated fresh mozzarella
2 Tablespoons sliced cherry peppers
2 Tablespoons diced roma tomatoes
2 Tablespoons chopped grilled onion
2 Tablespoons pitted and sliced
    kalamata olives
2 Tablespoons crumbled feta cheese
Salt and freshly ground black pepper
Chopped fresh basil for garnish

Use prepared single pizza such as Boboli® or
Pletza®, and brush with garlic oil. Sprinkle mozzarella over top surface, and add cherry peppers,
roma tomatoes, onions, olives and feta cheese.
Sprinkle with salt and pepper to taste, and bake
according to pizza crust directions. Garnish with
chopped fresh basil.

Lemon Mousse Napoleons

For the Lemon Mousse
1/4 teaspoon gelatin
5 Tablespoons lemon juice
5 egg yolks
1/2 Cup sugar, plus 2 Tablespoons
1 teaspoon salt
2 Tablespoons finely chopped lemon zest
2 Cups heavy cream
2 Tablespoons amaretto

Sprinkle gelatin over lemon juice, and let stand
for 5 minutes. Put egg yolks, sugar, lemon-gelatin
mixture and salt in a glass bowl over (not in) boiling water. Whisk mixture constantly until thick
and smooth, approximately 5 minutes. Remove
bowl from heat and continue to whisk until custard reaches room temperature. Stir in lemon zest
and reserve.

Beat heavy cream with 2 tablespoons sugar
until stiff peaks form. Fold in amaretto. Gently
fold whipped cream into lemon custard.
Refrigerate until ready to use.

To Make the Napoleons
1 package Pepperidge Farm® Puff Pastry
4 Tablespoons powdered (10X) sugar
6 twists of lemon zest

Line a baking sheet with parchment paper.
Lightly oil the paper. Place each sheet of puff pastry flat onto parchment. Cut pastry into 12 equal
rectangles, but do not move pieces. Bake according to package instructions. When cool split each
rectangle horizontally into 2 pieces.

To assemble use a spatula to place 1 piece of
pastry on each plate. Spoon lemon mousse on top.
Add a few blueberries (raspberries, strawberries
or a combination), and top with another piece of
pastry. Spoon more lemon mousse on top and a
few more berries. Repeat process to make 3 layers
ending with puff pastry. Sprinkle powdered sugar
through a fine-mesh strainer over the top of each
Napoleon, and garnish with a lemon twist.

Bass Baked in Parchment Paper

GIORGIOS
BAKATSIAS
CHEF-PROPRIETOR

Veteran Triangle restaurateur Giorgios Bakatsias is the talent behind this restaurant-cum-seafood store-cum-grill-cum-bakery and take-out market. Seafood is in the spotlight—fresh in the on-premise market to take home and cook yourself, or prepared to order in the restaurant. It's all there, in "The Garage" on Ninth Street in Durham.

Grilled Eggplant and Roasted Tomato Soup

1/2 Cup olive oil, divided
6 Japanese eggplants, sliced vertically
   into 1/4-inch slices
3 bulbs garlic
6 roma tomatoes
1 Tablespoon salt
Freshly ground black pepper to taste
1 1/4 Cups chopped onion
1/4 teaspoon curry powder
1 quart chicken stock
2 Tablespoons chopped fresh basil
2 Tablespoons fresh thyme leaves
1/4 teaspoon ground cumin
1 Tablespoon lemon juice
2 teaspoons freshly ground black pepper

Heat charcoal grill to medium hot. Oil eggplant slices on both sides, and grill until tender but not mushy, about 3 minutes per side. Remove eggplant from grill, cut into 3/4-inch cubes and reserve.

Cut a horizontal slice off the stem end of each garlic bulb. Pour a teaspoon of olive oil over each bulb, and wrap tightly in foil. Grill garlic, covered, for 30 minutes or until each clove is soft, and the cut surface of bulb is caramel colored. Remove, and reserve.

Cut tomatoes in half lengthwise, and season with salt, pepper and olive oil. Roast in a 375°F oven for 30 minutes or until edges begin to brown. Remove, and reserve.

Using a large soup pot over medium-low heat, sweat onions in 2 tablespoons olive oil until translucent, approximately 10 minutes. Add curry powder, and cook 1 minute. Add stock, fresh herbs, cumin, roasted tomatoes, lemon juice and eggplant cubes. Bring to a boil. Add salt and pepper, and simmer for 5 minutes. Serve with fresh crusty bread.

Bass Baked in Parchment Paper

3 lemons
6 pieces parchment paper
   (12- by 12-inches each)
6 8-ounce striped bass fillets
Salt and freshly ground black pepper
3/4 Cup olive oil
3/4 Cup white wine
12 sprigs fresh rosemary
6 sprigs fresh thyme

Slice lemons into 1/4-inch thick wheels and place an equal number on each piece of parchment paper. Place 1 fish fillet on top of each group of lemon wheels, and season with salt and pepper. Drizzle 2 tablespoons olive oil and 2 tablespoons white wine over each fillet. Top each fillet with 2 sprigs rosemary and 1 sprig thyme. Fold parchment to completely seal fish. Place parchment packages on a baking sheet, and bake at 400°F for 5 to 10 minutes, depending on thickness of fillets—allow approximately 10 minutes per inch of thickness. Serve, allowing each diner to open his own package.

Spicy Squid

2 pounds cleaned squid
4 roma tomatoes, coarsely chopped
1 red bell pepper, cut into 1/2-inch squares
2/3 Cup minced red onion
1 teaspoon minced garlic
1 Cup fresh lemon juice
10 sprigs Italian parsley, chopped
1/4 Cup extra virgin olive oil
2 teaspoons red pepper flakes
1/2 teaspoon dried oregano
Salt and freshly ground black pepper

Cut squid into rings, and set aside. Place tomatoes, red bell pepper, onion and garlic in a large mixing bowl, and set aside. Bring large pot of water to a boil, add 1 tablespoon salt for each 3 quarts water, and return to boil. Drop squid into boiling salted water, and cook for 8 to 10 minutes. Drain, and add cooked squid to mixing bowl with tomato mixture. Add lemon juice, parsley, olive oil, red pepper flakes and oregano. Toss to coat squid. Taste for seasoning, and adjust if necessary. Serve warm or at room temperature.

Grilled Whole Red Snapper

1 red snapper (4 1/2-pounds), cleaned
   and left whole
2 teaspoons ground fennel seeds
1 teaspoon whole mustard seeds
1 Cup olive oil, divided
Salt and freshly ground black pepper
12 vertical slices fresh zucchini, 1/4-inch thick
2 red bell peppers, seeded, cut into thirds
2 large (Beefsteak-type) fresh tomatoes,
   sliced into 1/4-inch thick slices
1 1/2 teaspoons fresh dill weed
1 teaspoon minced garlic
1/4 Cup lemon juice
Salt and freshly ground black pepper

Mix ground fennel, mustard seeds, salt and pepper with 3 tablespoons olive oil. Massage fish all over, including inside cavity, with mixture. Allow to rest for 15 minutes.

Heat charcoal fire to medium hot. Place fish on grill, and cook for about 15 minutes per side. When fish is turned to second side, sprinkle olive oil over zucchini, red bell pepper and tomato slices, and place on grill. Salt and pepper vegetables, and grill on both sides 15 minutes or until tender.

Whisk together dill, garlic, lemon juice and remaining olive oil. Add salt and freshly ground black pepper to taste. Reserve.

When fish is cooked through remove from grill, and place on large platter. Surround fish with grilled vegetables, and immediately pour reserved herbed olive oil over all. Serve immediately.

Pork Tenderloin with Sweet Papaya Mustard, Black Beans and Brown Rice

Pistachio-Crusted Grouper with Chipotle-Cilantro Butter and Pineapple Rum Salsa

MATTHEW SELENSKI
EXECUTIVE CHEF

The Glenwood Grill in Raleigh is a high-energy, friendly gathering place for the local "Old Raleigh" neighborhood clientele and newcomers alike.

Chef Matthew Selenski has a keen eye for colorful food presentations and a penchant for provocative taste combinations.

▼▼▼▼▼▼▼▼▼▼▼▼▼▼▼▼▼▼▼▼▼▼▼▼▼

Roasted Tomato, Red Pepper and Fresh Herb Soup

4 Cups chicken stock
8 large ripe tomatoes, cored and
    scored on bottom
4 large red bell peppers, top and
    seeds removed
2 Cups diced onion
2 Tablespoons olive oil
2 Tablespoons coarsely chopped fresh basil
2 Tablespoons chopped fresh oregano
2 Tablespoons chopped fresh thyme
1 Tablespoon minced garlic
1 Tablespoon chopped fresh chives
Salt and freshly ground black pepper
1 Cup heavy cream
1 Tablespoon cornstarch dissolved in
    2 Tablespoons cold water

Place tomatoes, core sides down, and red bell peppers, top sides down, on a baking sheet. Season with salt and pepper.

Pour chicken stock around tomatoes and bell peppers, and bake at 500°F for 30 minutes or until both tomatoes and peppers are soft. Remove from oven, and cool. Remove, and discard peel. Reserve both flesh and stock.

Sweat onions in olive oil until soft. Add garlic, roasted tomatoes, bell peppers and chicken stock. Heat to simmer, and add fresh herbs, except chives. Simmer for 10 minutes. Puree mixture in

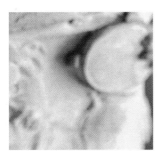

blender, and pass through sieve or fine-mesh strainer to remove seeds. Return to cooking pot, and add cream and cornstarch mixture. Stir with a wooden spoon until thickened, approximately 5 minutes. Garnish with chopped chives. May be served hot or cold.

Lump Crab Cakes with Green Mango Salsa

For the Crab Cakes
1/4 Cup diced tasso [See *Editor's Note*]
1/4 Cup diced green onions
1/4 Cup diced roasted red bell peppers
1/4 Cup finely chopped parsley
2 Tablespoons lemon juice
1 Tablespoon Dijon mustard
1 Tablespoon Worcestershire sauce
1 egg
1 Cup mayonnaise
1 teaspoon Old Bay Seasoning®
1 pound lump crabmeat
2 Cups fine breadcrumbs, divided
1/4 Cup oil for frying
12 ounces mixed baby greens

Combine all ingredients except crabmeat, breadcrumbs, frying oil and greens. Mix well. Fold in crabmeat, then 1 cup breadcrumbs. Form mixture into 6 cakes. Coat cakes with remaining breadcrumbs, and fry in small amount of oil in nonstick skillet. Brown each cake well on both sides and, if necessary, put in 400°F oven to hold while you fry any remaining cakes. Serve with Green Mango Salsa.

For the Green Mango Salsa
1 ripe mango, peeled, seeded and coarsely chopped
3 teaspoons minced fresh jalapeño
1 Cup chopped fresh cilantro leaves
3/4 Cup orange juice
1/4 Cup honey
1 Tablespoon rice wine vinegar
3/4 Cup peanut oil

Puree all ingredients except oil in blender, then with blender on low speed add oil in a slow, steady stream. Blend until thick and smooth. Set aside.

To Assemble
Place warm crab cake on a small bed of greens. Top with Green Mango Salsa.

Pistachio-Crusted Grouper with Chipotle-Cilantro Butter and Pineapple Rum Salsa

For the Chipotle-Cilantro Butter
8 Tablespoons (1 stick) butter, softened
1 teaspoon finely chopped chipotle chili pepper
3 Tablespoons chopped fresh cilantro leaves
1 Tablespoon fresh lime juice
Salt and freshly ground black pepper
Combine all ingredients in a bowl, and use a wooden spoon to mix until smooth. Reserve.

For the Grouper
6 grouper fillets (6-ounces each) other firm-fleshed white fish
Salt and freshly ground black pepper
2 egg whites, lightly beaten
1 Cup finely chopped pistachio nuts
1 Tablespoon olive oil
3/4 Cup white wine
Season each fillet with salt and pepper. Dip each piece of fish in beaten egg white then in pistachios. Press the pistachios to coat the fish evenly.

Heat olive oil over medium heat. When hot, add fish and lightly brown both sides. Remove, and place in an oven-proof dish. Add white wine, and cook in a 450°F oven for 10 minutes or until fish is firm and flesh is opaque in the center.

For the Pineapple Rum Salsa
1 ripe pineapple
1/4 Cup dark rum
1/4 Cup fresh orange juice
2 Tablespoons honey
2 Tablespoons soy sauce
2 Tablespoons rice wine vinegar
2 Tablespoons olive oil
1 red bell pepper, diced
1 teaspoon fresh lime juice
1 teaspoon chopped fresh mint leaves
Salt and freshly ground black pepper
Peel and core pineapple. Cut into 1 1/2-inch wedges. In a large glass bowl combine rum, orange juice, honey, soy sauce, rice vinegar and oil. Add pineapple wedges, and marinate for at least 30 minutes.

Heat charcoal grill or cast iron grill pan to

medium hot. Remove pineapple pieces, and reserve marinade. Lightly grill pineapple until grill marks are medium brown. Cool, and cut into small dice.

Combine pineapple, reserved marinade, red bell pepper, mint, lime juice, salt and pepper. Let rest at room temperature for 1 hour.

To Assemble

Put 1/2 cup of salsa in the middle of each plate. Place 1 fish fillet on top of salsa, and top with 1 tablespoon Chipotle-Cilantro Butter. Serve immediately.

Pork Tenderloin with Sweet Papaya Mustard, Black Beans and Brown Rice

For the Pork Tenderloin
    2 pounds pork tenderloin, trimmed
    1 Tablespoon peanut oil
Heat a skillet until very hot. Add peanut oil, and heat until almost smoking. Add tenderloins, and cook until meat is well browned on all sides, about 7 or 8 minutes. Remove from pan, and keep warm.

For the Sweet Papaya Mustard
    1 ripe papaya
    2 Tablespoons rice wine vinegar
    2 Tablespoons honey
    1/2 Cup orange juice
    2 Tablespoons whole-grain Dijon mustard
    1/2 teaspoon Jamaican jerk seasoning
        [See *Cook's Notes & Glossary*]
    1/2 teaspoon ground cumin
    1/2 teaspoon curry powder
    1/2 Cup olive oil
In a blender combine all ingredients except olive oil. Pulse on and off for 30 seconds. With blender running on medium speed add olive oil in a slow, steady stream until mixture is smooth and thick.

To Assemble
    2 Cups cooked brown rice
    2 Cups cooked black beans
    3 Tablespoons chicken stock
To serve heat rice and black beans in chicken stock. Place a large spoonful of rice and beans on each plate, top with slices of pork arranged in a fan, and top with Sweet Papaya Mustard.

Fresh Blackberry Linzertorte

    10 Tablespoons butter
    1/2 Cup sugar
    1 egg yolk
    1/2 Cup ground toasted almonds
    1/2 Cup ground walnuts
    1 teaspoon lemon zest
    2 Tablespoons lemon juice
    2 hard-boiled egg yolks, sieved
    1 1/4 Cups all-purpose flour
    1/2 teaspoon salt
    1/2 teaspoon cinnamon
    1/4 teaspoon ground cloves
    1 pint fresh blackberries
    1 Cup blackberry jam
    1 egg white beaten with 1 Tablespoon water
Beat butter and sugar until fluffy. Add raw egg yolk and incorporate well. Add ground nuts, lemon juice and lemon zest. Stir. Add sieved egg yolks, and mix well. Add flour, salt, cinnamon and cloves, and stir to combine.

Shape dough into a ball, and refrigerate for 1 hour. Reserve a quarter of the dough for lattice, and with floured hands press remaining dough into a 9-inch springform pan or tart pan with a removable bottom. Press dough to an even thickness on bottom of pan, and push up sides about 1/2 inch to form a small lip.

Mix fresh blackberries with blackberry jam. Be careful not to crush fresh berries. Pour blackberry mixture into crust. Put reserved dough into a pastry bag fitted with large round tip. Pipe dough in a lattice pattern over berries. Brush lattice lightly with egg and water mixture.

Bake in a pre-heated 350°F oven for 30 to 35 minutes or until crust is golden. Let cool completely before removing from pan.

Editor's Note
• *For tasso you can substitute trimmed country ham.*

Shepherd's Pie

PETER EDGAR
EXECUTIVE CHEF

Greenshields Brewery & Pub in Raleigh's City Market is renowned for its house-brewed beers. The decor in the bar is reminiscent of a British pub, as are many of the dishes on the menu. If you choose to eat in the Beer Garden you'll be surrounded by the sparkling brew-making equipment.

Beer and Cheese Soup

12 ounces amber beer
2 quarts chicken stock
3 teaspoons sugar
3/4 Cup butter
3/4 Cup all-purpose flour
1 Cup grated Cheddar cheese
1 Cup grated Monterey Jack cheese
2 Cups heavy cream
Chopped bacon bits and
    broccoli florets for garnish

Combine beer and chicken stock, and bring to a boil. Boil uncovered until reduced by half. Add sugar.

Melt butter in small sauté pan. Add flour, and stir with a wire whisk until a golden-colored roux is created.

Add roux to beer and chicken stock, whisking until well combined and soup thickens. Add Cheddar and Jack cheeses, and stir until smooth. Add cream, and stir.

Serve with chopped bacon bits and broccoli floret for garnish.

Sassafras-Smoked Shrimp with Roasted Corn Salsa

30 medium-size shrimp, shell on
1/2 Cup tequila
1/4 Cup fresh lime juice

Combine tequila and lime juice, pour over shrimp, and marinate for 30 minutes. Using a home smoker or kettle-style grill with hickory or applewood chips smoke shrimp until tender, about 20 minutes. Remove from grill, cool slightly, and peel.

For the Salsa

4 ears sweet corn
1 Cup peeled, seeded and diced
   roma tomatoes
2/3 Cup finely diced red onion
1/4 Cup chopped cilantro leaves
2 Tablespoons minced garlic
1 teaspoon ground cumin
1/4 Cup fresh lime juice
2 Tablespoons pure olive oil
1/2 teaspoon minced fresh jalapeño
2 Tablespoons balsamic vinegar
Salt and freshly ground black pepper

Using a charcoal grill or smoker roast corn over medium heat until evenly cooked, about 15 to 20 minutes. Remove kernels from cob, and combine with remaining ingredients. Let rest for 2 hours to reach full flavor. Serve salsa room temperature topped with smoked shrimp.

Shepherd's Pie

2 Tablespoons peanut oil, divided
3 1/2 Cups diced beef
3 Cups diced lamb
1 1/2 Cups diced red onion
1 Cup diced carrot
3/4 Cup frozen green peas
1/2 Cup frozen corn kernels
5 Tablespoons butter
2 Tablespoons flour
1 1/2 Cups beef stock
Salt and freshly ground black pepper
3 Cups mashed potatoes (about 6 potatoes)

Brown beef and lamb cubes in 1 tablespoon peanut oil. Drain, and reserve. Sauté onion and carrot in remaining tablespoon peanut oil until tender, about 5 minutes. Add browned beef, lamb, peas and corn to onion and carrot mixture.

In a medium saucepan combine butter and flour, and cook until bubbly. Add beef stock, and cook until thickened. Season with salt and pepper. Pour sauce over beef and lamb mixture. Pour mixture into 9- by 13-inch dish, and top with mashed potatoes piped through a pastry bag with a large star tip. Bake in a 350°F oven for 30 minutes or until potatoes are a golden brown.

Chicken Breasts in Marsala Mushroom Sauce

3 whole skinless, boneless chicken breasts, each cut in half
3 Tablespoons butter
2 Tablespoons vegetable oil
3/4 Cup minced shallots
3/4 Cup sliced shiitake mushrooms
3/4 Cup sliced cremini mushrooms
1 Cup Marsala
3/4 Cup chicken stock
1/2 Cup sour cream
Salt and freshly ground black pepper
1 Tablespoon chopped fresh rosemary
2 Tablespoons chopped parsley

Gently pound each piece of chicken to uniform thickness.

In a large sauté pan that will hold all chicken pieces in one layer, melt oil and 1 tablespoon butter. When butter foam subsides add shallots and mushrooms, and sauté until tender, about 5 minutes. Remove shallots and mushrooms from pan, and keep warm.

Add remaining butter to skillet, and heat until foaming. Add chicken breasts, and sauté 4 to 5 minutes per side or until lightly browned. Add Marsala, and bring to a boil, scraping brown bits from bottom of pan. Remove chicken from pan, and keep warm. Add chicken stock to pan, and bring to a boil. Lower heat until liquid is no longer boiling. Add sour cream, shallot and mushroom mixture and fresh rosemary. Simmer 5 minutes. Do not boil or sauce will separate.

Place chicken breasts on platter, and top with sauce. Garnish with chopped fresh parsley.

English Trifle

12 ounces Sara Lee® pound cake, cubed (about 3 Cups)
1 package instant French vanilla pudding mix
1 1/4 Cups half-and-half
1 1/4 Cups whole milk
1 jar (10-ounce) strawberry preserves
1/4 Cup dry sherry
1 Tablespoon macaroon cookie crumbs
Whipped cream and strawberries for garnish

Using a whisk combine pudding mix, cream and milk. Chill to set.

Using a straight-sided glass bowl form a layer of pound cake cubes in bottom. Put sherry in spray bottle and spray cake cubes. Warm strawberry preserves in microwave, and drizzle 1 tablespoon of preserves over cake. Spoon a third of chilled pudding on top of preserves. Repeat layering procedure ending with pudding. Sprinkle macaroon cookie crumbs over top, and refrigerate for 4 to 6 hours. Serve with freshly whipped cream and fresh strawberries for garnish.

Tomato and Arugula Salad

BRIAN STAPLETON
EXECUTIVE CHEF

Il Palio Ristorante in The Siena Hotel in Chapel Hill, is the only AAA Four-Diamond Italian restaurant in North Carolina. Chef Brian Stapleton's Tuscan cuisine and award-winning wine list make Il Palio a favorite spot for visitors and local clientele alike.

▼▼▼▼▼▼▼▼▼▼▼▼▼▼▼▼▼▼▼▼▼▼▼▼▼▼▼

Potato and Celeriac Soup

1 1/2 Cups trimmed,
   coarsely chopped country ham
1 1/2 Cups coarsely chopped celeriac
   [See *Editor's Note*]
1 3/4 Cups coarsely chopped onion
1 1/2 Tablespoons diced garlic
6 Cups chicken stock
5 Cups coarsely chopped potatoes
1 teaspoon freshly ground black pepper
1 Cup half-and-half
Fresh-snipped chives for garnish

Heat a deep soup pot on high heat for 1 minute. Add country ham, and sauté until crisp. Add celeriac, onions and garlic, and sauté until onions are translucent. Add chicken stock, and bring to a boil. Add potatoes and pepper, and boil until soft, about 15 minutes.

Divide soup into batches, and blend in food processor or blender until smooth. Strain into a clean pot. Thin soup with half-and-half to desired consistency. Garnish with fresh-snipped chives.

Tomato and Arugula Salad

3 bunches fresh arugula, well-cleaned
3 medium-size, vine-ripened tomatoes
18 kalamata olives, pitted and sliced
1 large Bermuda onion, thinly sliced
1/4 Cup balsamic vinegar
3/4 Cup olive oil
2 teaspoons minced garlic
1 Tablespoon sugar
Salt and freshly ground black pepper

Using a whisk and a glass bowl, combine vinegar, oil, garlic, sugar, salt and pepper.

Arrange arugula on each plate, top each with onion, tomato and olive slices. Drizzle each portion with dressing, and serve immediately.

Eggplant Gnocchi with Oregano-Mascarpone Sauce

Note: this recipe requires a food mill to process the potatoes and eggplant. Substituting a food processor or blender will create a mixture that is too sticky.

1 medium-size eggplant, peeled and sliced
3 Tablespoons olive oil
Salt and freshly ground black pepper
1 pound russet potatoes, peeled and
    coarsely chopped
1 3/4 Cups all-purpose flour
1 egg, slightly beaten

Season eggplant slices with olive oil, salt and pepper. Grill over medium heat until tender. Set aside.

Steam potatoes until soft but not mushy, approximately 10 minutes. Set aside while you sift flour into large bowl, and add beaten egg. Using a food mill, process eggplant and potato together into flour. Season with salt and pepper.

Use hands to mix gnocchi batter and to roll mixture into a 1/2-inch diameter log or stick. Chill. When ready to cook cut log into 1/2-inch long pieces. Cook in boiling salted water until gnocchi rise to the top. Carefully lift gnocchi out of water with a slotted spoon, and place on a platter. Blot platter with paper towels to remove any excess liquid. Cover with sauce.

For the Sauce
2 Tablespoons butter, divided
2 Tablespoons diced shallots
1 teaspoon minced garlic
1 Cup chicken stock
1/4 teaspoon dried oregano
1/4 Cup mascarpone cheese
1 Tablespoon Parmesan cheese

Melt 1 tablespoon butter in sauté pan over medium-high heat. Sauté shallots and garlic for 3 minutes. Add chicken stock, and reduce by half. Add oregano, cheeses and remaining butter, and whisk until combined. Pour over warm gnocchi and serve immediately.

Filetto di Branzino

(Spinach-Stuffed Grouper Fillets with Prosciutto and Fresh Vegetables)

For the Saffron Broth

    6 to 8 saffron threads
    2 bay leaves
    5 black peppercorns
    2 stalks lemon grass
    2 Tablespoons minced fresh ginger
    1 Tablespoon chopped shallots
    1 teaspoon minced garlic
    3 Cups water

Combine saffron, bay leaves, peppercorns, lemon grass, ginger, shallots and garlic in water. Bring to simmer, and cook for 10 minutes. Remove from heat, cover, and let steep for 20 minutes.

For the Fish

    28 ounces skinned, boned black grouper fillet
    1/2 pound Asian greens
    12 slices prosciutto ham
    1 Tablespoon pure olive oil
    1 Tablespoon butter
    1/2 Cup julienned zucchini
    1/2 Cup julienned leek
    1/3 Cup julienned daikon radish
    1/2 Cup julienned red onion
    3 Cups cooked orzo pasta

Butterfly grouper fillets. Place a handful of greens in middle of each fillet, and roll fish around greens so that greens are in the center. Wrap outside of fish with prosciutto slices.

Heat a non-stick skillet over medium-high heat. Add 1 tablespoon vegetable oil, and sear fish on all sides for 1 minute. Transfer fish to baking dish, and cook in 350°F oven for 10 minutes.

While fish is baking, cook julienned vegetables in butter and 1 teaspoon saffron broth until *al dente*.

To Assemble

Place 1/2 cup of cooked orzo on each of 6 plates. Top with braised vegetables. Cut fish diagonally to expose greens, and place on top of vegetables. Pour saffron broth around presentation, and serve immediately.

Orange Mango Gelato

    3 ripe mangoes, peeled, seeded and
       coarsely chopped
    1 1/2 Cups orange juice concentrate
    1/3 Cup water
    1/3 Cup Triple Sec
    1/3 Cup sugar

Place all ingredients in blender, and puree on high speed for approximately 2 minutes. Transfer to a freezer container, cover, and freeze for at least 14 hours.

Editor's Note
• *Celeriac is a knobby, brown vegetable cultivated especially for its root. It is also called celery root or celery knob, and is available in the winter months. Celeriac's flavor is a combination of strong celery and parsley. If celeriac is unavailable, substitute 1 1/2 cups chopped celery rib and 3 tablespoons chopped Italian parsley, including the parsley stems.*

Black and White Ying/Yang Beans with Mango Salsa

Peach Cobbler

ARTHUR GORDON
CHEF-PROPRIETOR

Irregardless Cafe in Raleigh was one of the first restaurants in the Triangle to present a vegetarian-inspired, pro-health menu. The menu is now broadened to incorporate some meat and fish dishes, but it retains the special care and creativity of chef-proprietor Arthur Gordon.

Cauliflower Soup

2 Tablespoons butter, divided
1 Cup diced onion
2 ribs celery, minced
2/3 Cup diced carrot
2 Tablespoons all-purpose flour
8 Cups vegetable stock, divided
4 Cups diced cauliflower florets
1 bay leaf
1/2 teaspoon dried tarragon
Salt and freshly ground pepper to taste
1/2 Cup milk

Melt 1 tablespoon butter in sauté pan, and add onions, celery and carrots. Sauté for 4 minutes, then add flour and 1/4 cup stock. Cook 30 seconds, stirring constantly. Add cauliflower, and cook over low heat for 2 minutes. Add bay leaf and 6 cups stock. Simmer 15 minutes or until cauliflower is tender.

Boil remaining stock in small saucepan. Add tarragon. Remove from heat, and cover. Let stand 5 minutes. Uncover, and strain liquid into soup, discarding tarragon. Add salt, pepper and milk.

Spanakopita

2 10-ounce packages frozen spinach
1 Cup chopped onion
1 Tablespoon olive oil
1 1/2 teaspoons minced garlic
8 Tablespoons (1 stick) butter, divided
3 Tablespoons all-purpose flour
1/4 Cup Romano cheese
1 pound ricotta cheese
4 ounces cream cheese
4 eggs, beaten
3 teaspoons salt
1/2 teaspoon freshly ground black pepper
1 package phyllo pastry, thawed
[See *Cook's Notes & Glossary*]

Thaw and squeeze spinach as dry as possible, saving 1/2 cup of juice.

Heat a skillet over medium-high heat, and add olive oil. Add onions, and sauté until limp and glossy. Add garlic, and cook for 1 minute. Add flour and 3 tablespoons butter, and stir constantly for 3 minutes. Add reserved spinach juice, and cook until thickened. Add chopped spinach, cheeses, and stir well. Remove from heat, and add eggs and salt. Combine well. Reserve.

Remove phyllo from package, and unfold. Keep pastry covered, first with sheet of plastic wrap, then damp towel. Contact with air will cause pastry to dry out and crumble.

Melt remaining 5 tablespoons butter. Lightly oil bottom of a 9- by 13-inch baking pan. Place 3 sheets of phyllo on bottom, and brush top of pastry liberally with melted butter. Top with one third of spinach mixture. Place 3 more sheets of pastry on top, and brush with butter. Add second third of spinach mixture. Repeat process ending with pastry brushed with butter. Bake in 350°F oven for 30 to 45 minutes or until pastry is golden and flaky. Cool, cut into squares and serve.

Black and White Ying/Yang Beans with Mango Salsa

For the White Beans
1 Cup dried great Northern beans,
    cooked according to package directions
2 teaspoons peanut oil
1 Cup chopped onion
2 teaspoons minced garlic
1/4 Cup fresh lime juice
1 1/2 Cups diced zucchini
Salt and freshly ground black pepper
1 Cup frozen green peas, thawed

In a sauté pan over medium heat, heat oil until hot. Add onion and garlic, and cook until tender. Add lime juice, zucchini, salt and pepper. Add cooked beans and green peas, mix well and set aside.

For the Black Beans
2 teaspoons olive oil
1 Cup chopped onion
2 teaspoons minced garlic
1/4 Cup lemon juice
2/3 Cup diced carrots
1 Cup diced cooked beets
Salt and freshly ground black pepper

In a sauté pan over medium heat, heat oil until hot. Add onion and garlic, and cook until tender. Add lemon juice, carrots and beets, and cook over low heat for 15 minutes until vegetables take on a neon look, (you'll know it when you see it). Salt and pepper to taste, and set aside.

For the Mango Salsa
2 mangoes, peeled, seeded and diced
1 Tablespoon fresh lemon juice
1 Tablespoon fresh lime juice
Pinch salt
Pinch sugar
Pinch cayenne pepper
1/4 Cup minced red bell pepper

Combine all ingredients in a glass bowl, and set aside.

For the Yellow Rice
3 Cups water
2 Cups long-grain brown rice
1 Tablespoon tumeric (or pinch of saffron)
1 teaspoon salt

In a pot with tight-fitting lid bring water to a boil, and add rice, tumeric and salt. Reduce heat to a simmer, and cover. Cook 20 minutes. (Do not stir or remove lid.) Remove from heat, and let stand for 20 minutes undisturbed.

To Assemble

Make a vertical stripe of yellow rice in the middle of each plate. Place portion of black bean mixture on one side of rice and a portion of white bean mixture on other side of rice. Top each presentation with mango salsa, and serve immediately.

Tuna Kilimanjaro

6 tuna fillets (6-ounces each),
　blood line removed
6 Tablespoons dill butter or garlic butter
　[See *Cook's Notes & Glossary*]

For the Cashews

1 Cup water
1/4 teaspoon Texas Pete® hot sauce
1 teaspoon soy sauce
1 Cup cashews

Bring water, hot sauce and soy sauce to a boil. Add cashews, and cook for 3 minutes. Drain nuts, and discard liquid. Place nuts on baking sheet, and roast in 350°F oven for 25 minutes. Cool. Grind nuts in food processor. Reserve.

For the Coating

1 Cup coarsely chopped celery
1 Cup chopped onion
1 red bell pepper, seeded and chopped
1/3 Cup lemon juice
1/3 Cup tahini
　[See *Cook's Notes & Glossary*]
1 Cup roasted, crushed cashew nuts
　(recipe above)
1 Cup cracker crumbs
Vegetable oil for sautéing

Puree celery, pepper and onion in a food processor or blender. Add lemon juice, tahini, cashews and cracker crumbs, and mix well.

To Cook Fish

Pat tuna fillets on both sides with coating, and sauté fish in peanut or vegetable oil for approximately 10 minutes per inch of thickness of fillets. Turn only once. When done serve with a pat of dill butter or garlic butter.

Peach Cobbler

1/2 pound (2 sticks) salted butter
2 1/2 Cups sugar, divided
1/2 teaspoon salt
2 Cups whole milk
1/2 teaspoon vanilla extract
2 Cups plus 2 Tablespoons sifted
　all-purpose flour
12 Cups peeled, pitted and diced peaches
1/4 Cup peach liqueur (optional)

Using an electric mixer on medium-high speed, cream butter, 2 cups sugar and salt until fluffy, about 8 minutes. Reduce speed to low, and slowly add milk and vanilla. When combined slowly add 2 cups flour. Beat for 5 minutes on medium-high speed.

Toss peaches with remaining 1/2 cup sugar, 2 tablespoons flour and liqueur. Arrange peaches in a 9- by 13-inch greased, oven-proof dish. Pour batter over peaches, and bake in a 350°F oven for 1 hour. Cobbler is done when top is brown and a toothpick inserted in the middle comes out clean.

Bow Tie Pasta with Basil Oregano Sauce

**VIVIAN JONES
CHEF &
CO-PROPRIETOR**

Jovi's Cafe is located in a lovely old house on a side street in Wake Forest. Presided over by co-owners Vivian Jones and her sister, Jonnie Anderson, Jovi's engenders that warm feeling of Southern hospitality offered in an unpretentious home-like atmosphere. Chef Vivian's cuisine remains true to the teachings of her mother—simple Southern fare with great flavor, graciously presented.

Potato Soup

4 Cups coarsely chopped potatoes
4 Cups water
1 teaspoon salt
1/2 teaspoon freshly ground black pepper
4 Tablespoons butter
2 Tablespoons all-purpose flour
3 Cups milk
1 Cup heavy cream

Place potatoes, water, salt, pepper and butter in a large saucepan. Cover, and bring to a quick boil. Reduce heat to simmer, and cook until potatoes are tender, approximately 10 minutes.

Mix flour with just enough water to make a runny smooth paste, add to potato mixture and cook for 1 minute. Add milk and cream, and cook 10 to 15 minutes stirring occasionally.

Bow Tie Pasta with Basil Oregano Sauce

For the Basil Oregano Sauce
>3/4 Cup packed fresh basil leaves
>1/4 Cup packed fresh oregano leaves
>1 teaspoon chopped garlic
>2 1/2 Cups olive oil
>1/4 Cup lemon juice
>1 Tablespoon white wine vinegar
>2 teaspoons salt
>1 1/2 teaspoons freshly ground black pepper

In a blender puree basil, oregano, garlic, olive oil, lemon juice and vinegar. Season well with salt and pepper.

For the Bow Tie Pasta
>1 pound bow tie pasta
>1 Tablespoon butter
>1/2 pound sliced mushrooms

Cook pasta in boiling salted water according to package instructions. While pasta is cooking, sauté mushrooms in butter.

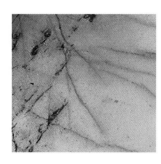

To Assemble
>Divide pasta among 6 serving bowls. Sprinkle an equal portion of mushrooms over each pasta serving, and pour basil oregano sauce over all.

Peppercorn Pork

>3 pounds pork loin
>1/3 Cup black peppercorns, coarsely ground

Completely cover pork loin with cracked peppercorns. Press pepper firmly in place to ensure it sticks to meat. Place pork in baking pan, and add just enough water to cover bottom of pan. Roast in a 375°F oven for approximately 1 hour or until a meat thermometer inserted into the center of the meat registers 155°F. Remove pork from pan, and allow to rest for 15 minutes before serving.

For the Sauce
>2 scallions, sliced (including green tops)
>1 Tablespoon all-purpose flour
>3 Tablespoons red wine

Scrape all juices and drippings from baking pan into a small saucepan. Bring to a boil, and add scallions. Cook for 1 minute. Add flour to wine, and whisk to combine. Add wine to pan, and boil for 1 minute. Serve over sliced pork.

Black Strawberry Cake

For the Cake
>1 Cup all-purpose flour
>1 Cup sugar
>1/8 teaspoon baking powder
>1/8 teaspoon baking soda
>1 teaspoon salt
>1/3 cup softened stick margarine
>   (not tub style)
>2 ounces (squares) unsweetened chocolate, melted
>1/2 Cup water
>1 teaspoon vanilla extract
>2 eggs

Combine flour, sugar, baking powder, baking soda, salt, margarine, melted chocolate, water and vanilla in large mixing bowl. Using an electric mixer on medium speed beat 2 minutes. Add eggs, and beat additional 2 minutes.

Pour batter into 2 greased, floured 8-inch cake pans. Bake at 350°F for 15 to 18 minutes or until toothpick inserted in middle of cake comes out clean. Cool cake in pans 10 minutes. Remove cake from pans, and allow to cool completely on cake racks.

For the Filling
>3/4 Cup chocolate chips
>2 Tablespoons margarine
>1 Tablespoon water
>25 strawberries, cleaned, tops removed

Melt chocolate chips and margarine over low heat. Add water, and stir. Dip strawberries in warm chocolate, completely covering the berries. Place on waxed paper to harden, approximately 10 minutes. Refrigerate.

For the Strawberry Puree
>15 to 20 strawberries
>3 Tablespoons powdered (10X) sugar
>Place all ingredients in blender, and pulse on and off until pureed. Reserve.

To Assemble

    1 1/2 Cups heavy cream, whipped until stiff

Spread half the whipped cream over bottom cake layer, leaving approximately 1/4 inch around edges. Place chocolate covered strawberries close together in whipped cream completely covering cake layer. Top with remainder of whipped cream. Place second layer on top, and put cake in refrigerator while you prepare ganache.

For the Ganache

    6 ounces bittersweet chocolate,
        coarsely chopped
    1/2 Cup heavy cream

Heat cream to a boil, and immediately pour over chopped chocolate. Let sit for 2 minutes, then stir until smooth.

    Pour ganache in a thin layer over top of cake, and allow it to drizzle down the sides. Continue pouring thin layers of ganache until it is all used. Serve cake with strawberry puree.

▼▼▼▼▼▼▼▼▼▼▼▼▼▼▼▼▼▼▼▼▼▼▼▼▼▼

Chocolate Finesse Cake

For the Cake Layers

    2 Cups all-purpose flour
    2 Cups sugar
    3/4 Cup shortening
    1 teaspoon baking soda
    2/3 Cup unsweetened cocoa powder
    1/2 teaspoon salt
    1 1/4 Cups whole milk, divided
    3/4 teaspoon baking powder
    3 eggs
    1 teaspoon vanilla extract

Grease and flour 2 8-inch cake pans and set aside.

    Using an electric mixer on medium speed beat flour, sugar, shortening, baking soda, cocoa, salt and 3/4 cup of milk for 2 minutes. Scrape sides of bowl as needed. Add baking powder, remaining milk, eggs and vanilla, and blend for 2 minutes on medium-high speed, scraping the sides of the bowl several times.

    Pour batter evenly into cake pans. Bake at

350°F for 35 to 40 minutes or until cake begins to pull away from sides of pan. Remove pans from oven, and place on a rack for 5 minutes to cool. Remove layers from pans, and cool completely on rack.

For the Filling

    1 pound very firm ricotta cheese
    1/4 Cup sugar
    3 Tablespoons dark rum, such as Myers's®
    3/4 Cup chocolate chips, chopped

Combine and beat ricotta, sugar, and rum until smooth. Stir in chocolate chips, and chill.

For the Icing

    6 ounces chocolate chips
    1/3 Cup very hot coffee
    4 egg yolks
    2 Tablespoons dark rum
    8 Tablespoons (1 stick) softened butter

Put chocolate chips and hot coffee into blender, and blend on high speed for about 20 seconds or until smooth. Add egg yolks and rum, and blend until combined. Drop butter into blender container a piece at a time, and blend on high speed for 2 minutes or until smooth and glossy. In warm weather you may need to chill this icing before spreading it on the cake.

To Assemble the Cake

    Cut each layer in half horizontally. Divide filling between layers. Spread buttercream icing on top and sides of cake. Refrigerate until ready to serve. This cake is best if made one day ahead.

Tuna on Summer Tomato and Basil Salad

MICHAEL SEESE
CHEF

Chefs Michael Seese and Jackie Derey preside over the kitchen in this charming Chapel Hill restaurant. La Res, as some of the locals call it, carries on the tradition of beautifully presented fine food, that was established by Bill Neal and his wife Moreton when they first opened La Residence in 1976.

▼▼▼▼▼▼▼▼▼▼▼▼▼▼▼▼▼▼▼▼▼▼▼▼▼▼▼▼▼▼

Fennel and Red Pepper Soup

1/2 Cup diced red pepper, plus extra
    for garnish
1/4 Cup chopped green bell pepper
3 Tablespoons olive oil, divided
1/2 Cup chopped onion
1 garlic clove
1 fennel bulb, coarsely chopped
2 Tablespoons all-purpose flour
2 1/2 Cups chicken stock
1/2 Tablespoon ground fennel seeds
1/2 teaspoon red pepper flakes
1 bay leaf
1/4 teaspoon dried thyme
2 canned tomatoes, seeded and chopped
Salt and freshly ground black pepper
3/4 Cup half-and-half

Sauté bell peppers in 1 tablespoon olive oil until tender. Remove from pan and reserve. Add remaining olive oil, onion, garlic and fennel, and sauté over medium-high heat until tender, about 3 to 5 minutes. Sprinkle flour over vegetables and stir. Cook for 2 minutes. Add stock, spices and tomatoes, and bring to a boil. Lower heat to a simmer, and cook for 20 to 30 minutes. Remove bay leaf, and puree soup in food processor. Pour through a fine-mesh strainer, and discard the solids. Add cream, salt and pepper, and heat through. Serve garnished with chopped red pepper and fennel tops.

Mesclun Salad with Roasted Peppers and Kalamata Olives

1 pound mixed baby greens (mesclun)
36 kalamata olives
1/2 Cup red wine vinegar
1 Tablespoon minced shallots
1 teaspoon minced fresh thyme leaves
1 1/2 Cups olive oil
3 medium-size red bell peppers, roasted, peeled and julienned into 1/8-inch strips
Salt and freshly ground black pepper

Place olives in an uncovered pan, and roast in a 400°F oven for 10 minutes. Remove pan from oven, cool and pit olives. Set aside.

Mix vinegar, shallots and thyme in a medium-size mixing bowl. While whisking constantly, add olive oil in a slow, steady stream. Whisk until mixture thickens. Mix greens in a salad bowl, add salt, pepper, red peppers and kalamata olives. Add dressing, toss, and serve.

Grilled Tuna on Summer Tomato and Basil Salad

For the Salad
3 Cups diced, peeled and seeded plum tomatoes
2/3 Cup diced red onion
1/2 Cup fresh basil chiffonade [See *Cook's Notes & Glossary*]
1 Tablespoon minced garlic
1/4 Cup diced shallots
2/3 Cup cooked pearl barley
1 teaspoon salt
1 teaspoon freshly ground black pepper
1/2 Cup balsamic vinegar
1 Cup extra virgin olive oil

Mix tomatoes, onion, basil chiffonade, garlic, shallots, barley, salt and pepper. Add oil and vinegar and set aside for 1 hour. Drain, and divide into 6 equal portions. Place each portion in a circular mold, such as a small biscuit cutter, in middle of each plate. Press down on mixture to compact it, then remove mold. Continue until all six salads are completed.

For the Tuna
6 fresh tuna fillets (6-ounces each)
Grill tuna over hot charcoal until medium-rare.

For the Garnish
1/4 Cup pure olive oil
18 fresh basil leaves
1 Cup balsamic vinegar

Heat olive oil in a heavy-bottom skillet. When hot add basil leaves and flash fry until crisp, about 1 minute. Remove leaves from pan, and set aside on paper towels to drain.

Place vinegar in a medium-size saucepan over high heat. Boil until reduced to a syrup. Set aside.

For the Dressing
1 Cup fresh basil leaves
1/2 Cup fresh Italian parsley leaves
1/2 Cup extra virgin olive oil
Pinch of salt

Blanch basil in 2 cups boiling water for 10 seconds. Remove and drain. Blanch parsley in same water for 10 seconds. Remove and drain. Add blanched herbs and olive oil to blender and process on high speed until oil turns green. Add salt and process for 10 seconds.

To Assemble
Top each portion of formed salad with grilled tuna fillet. Arrange 3 fried basil leaves on top of each fillet, and drizzle balsamic syrup around plate. Drizzle green herb oil around salad and plate, and serve.

Duck Breast with Port Wine Roquefort Sauce

6 boneless duck breasts (6-ounces each)
3 teaspoons salt
1 1/2 teaspoons freshly ground black pepper
1/2 teaspoon ground cloves
1/2 teaspoon ground allspice
1/2 teaspoon ground nutmeg
1/2 teaspoon ground cinnamon
1 Cup chopped carrots
1 Cup chopped onions
1 Cup chopped celery
3 cloves garlic
2 Tablespoons olive oil
1 Cup tawny port
1 Cup raspberry vinegar
3 bay leaves
1 teaspoon black peppercorns
1/4 teaspoon ground thyme

1/2 gallon duck or chicken stock
1/2 Cup all-purpose flour
8 Tablespoons (1 stick) butter

Score fat side of each duck breast with slits about 1/2-inch apart. Mix salt, pepper, cloves, allspice, nutmeg and cinnamon and pat on flesh side of each breast. Stack breasts, place in a plastic bag, and refrigerate 4 hours or overnight.

In a skillet over medium-high heat, sauté carrots, onions, celery, and garlic in olive oil until caramelized. Add port and vinegar, bay leaves, peppercorns and thyme to skillet and cook until liquid is reduced by two thirds. Strain and set aside.

Combine flour and butter in a skillet and whisk over medium heat until a golden roux forms. Bring stock to a boil and add roux, whisking to combine. Reduce liquid until thick enough to coat back of a spoon. Pour through a fine-mesh strainer, and set aside.

Remove duck breasts from plastic bag, and pat dry. Place breasts, fat side down, in a hot skillet and sauté until fat is rendered. Turn breasts and brown flesh side for about 5 minutes, or until medium-rare.

To Assemble
1 stick unsalted butter
1/2 Cup Roquefort cheese

Mix butter and cheese until well blended.

Combine stock mixture and vegetable-port mixture and heat to boiling. Slowly incorporate Roquefort butter and return to boil for 5 minutes. Sauce will turn dark and thicken. Keep over low heat.

Remove duck breasts from pan, slice and drizzle with port sauce.

Lemon Almond Torte

For the Torte
10 ounces unblanched almonds
2 Tablespoons lemon zest
1 1/3 Cups sugar, divided
1/3 Cup all-purpose flour
8 egg whites
1/2 teaspoon salt
1/4 teaspoon almond extract

Combine almonds and lemon zest, and process in food processor until finely ground. Add 2/3 cup sugar and flour and process until well combined.

Beat egg whites until soft peaks form. Add salt and almond extract, and combine well. Fold whites into almond mixture.

Butter and flour a 10-inch springform pan. Pour batter into pan and bake in a 350°F oven for 30 minutes. Decrease temperature to 300°F and bake 20 minutes more or until knife inserted in center of torte comes out clean. Remove from oven and let cool.

For the Lemon Curd Topping
3 whole eggs
1 egg yolk
1 Cup sugar
1/3 Cup fresh lemon juice
1 Tablespoon grated lemon rind
6 Tablespoons butter, at room temperature

Thoroughly mix whole eggs and egg yolks. Push through a medium-mesh strainer to remove any lumps. In a bowl over hot water, add sugar, lemon juice and lemon rind, then egg mixture. Stir with wooden spoon while mixture warms. When mixture begins to thicken add butter, one tablespoon at a time. Incorporate each tablespoon before adding the next. When all butter is fully incorporated and mixture is thick remove from heat and cool by placing bowl in another bowl filled with ice.

To Assemble
Slice cooled cake in half horizontally. Place one layer on serving plate and top with one third lemon custard topping. Place other half on top and spread remaining topping over top and sides of cake.

Sour Cream Apple Pie

NANCY QUAINTANCE EXECUTIVE CHEF

Lucky 32 in Raleigh is the sister establishment of restaurants in Greensboro and Winston-Salem of the same name—a lucky race car number. Executive chef, Nancy Quaintance has a particular flair for developing menus with diversity, and delicious specials from the many culinary regions around the world.

▼▼▼▼▼▼▼▼▼▼▼▼▼▼▼▼▼▼▼▼▼▼▼▼▼▼▼

Creamy Sweet Onion Soup

3 Tablespoons butter
6 Cups thinly sliced and quartered onions
1 teaspoon fresh lemon juice
2 teaspoons dry white wine
4 Cups chicken stock
1/2 teaspoon dried thyme
1 teaspoon minced garlic
3/4 teaspoon white pepper
1 1/2 teaspoons salt
1 Cup water
1/3 Cup roux [See *Cook's Notes & Glossary*]
2/3 Cup half-and-half

Melt butter in a large soup pot over medium-high heat. Add onions, and sauté until caramelized, about 15 minutes. Add lemon juice, white wine and chicken stock. Cook for 5 minutes. Add thyme, garlic, pepper, salt and water. Simmer, partially-covered, on medium-low heat for 30 minutes.

Take 1/2 cup of simmering soup liquid and add it to roux, whisking to incorporate. Add mixture back to pot of simmering soup, whisking until fully incorporated. Cook over medium-high heat approximately 15 minutes until thickened. Add cream, mix well, and serve.

Artichoke Dip

2 cans (14 1/2-ounces each) artichoke hearts
1/2 Cup mayonnaise
3/4 Cup sour cream
1/2 Cup grated Parmesan cheese,
 plus extra for garnish
1 1/2 teaspoons dried thyme
3/4 teaspoons fresh ground black pepper
1/4 teaspoon Tabasco® Sauce
Chopped parsley for garnish

Drain artichoke hearts, squeezing water out by hand. Using an electric mixer on low speed beat artichoke hearts until coarsely chopped. Add remaining ingredients, slowly increasing speed, until thoroughly blended. Put in 8- by 8-inch glass pan and bake in 375°F oven until bubbly and hot throughout, approximately 15 to 20 minutes. Sprinkle with additional Parmesan and chopped parsley, and serve warm with crackers.

Ham and Pork Loaf with Two-Mustard Sauce

1 1/2 pounds pork loin
1 1/2 pounds Hormel Cure 81 Ham®
1 1/2 Cups fresh breadcrumbs
5 Tablespoons whole-grain mustard
1 Tablespoon melted clarified butter
1 1/4 teaspoons freshly ground black pepper
3 eggs
Scant Cup milk

Spray one large or two small loaf pans with Pam® or other spray shortening. Set aside.

Trim excess fat from pork loin, and cut into 1-inch chunks. Cut ham into 1-inch chunks. Place both meats in food processor, and process until finely ground. Transfer pork mixture to large bowl, and add remaining ingredients. Use hands to blend ingredients well. Put mixture into prepared loaf pan(s) and bake in 350°F oven for 1 1/2 hours or until internal temperature reaches 150°F. Spread top with 2 tablespoons Two-Mustard Sauce, and bake for 10 more minutes. Remove from oven, glaze meatloaf with additional Two-Mustard Sauce. Cool, slice and serve with additional Two Mustard Sauce on the side.

For the Two-Mustard Sauce
 1 Cup packed brown sugar
 3 Tablespoons powdered mustard
 1 Cup cider vinegar
 1 Cup prepared whole-grain mustard

Combine all ingredients, and mix well.

White Bean Crostini

For The Sage-Cooked White Beans
>   1 pound dried white beans
>   (great Northern or cannellini)
>   1 1/2 Tablespoons olive oil
>   1 teaspoon chopped fresh garlic
>   1/4 Cup chopped fresh sage leaves
>   6 1/2 Cups chicken stock
>   1/4 teaspoon salt
>   Pinch freshly ground black pepper

Wash and soak beans for 6 to 8 hours. Drain.

In a large pot over medium-high heat, sauté garlic in olive oil until translucent. Add beans, sage and stock. Lower heat, and simmer for 40 to 45 minutes until beans are tender, but remain firm. Do not overcook. Remove beans from heat, and drain. Season with salt and pepper. This may be done ahead and refrigerated until needed.

To Assemble
>   1 Tablespoon balsamic vinegar
>   1/4 teaspoon freshly ground black pepper
>   1/2 teaspoon salt
>   3 Tablespoons extra virgin olive oil, divided
>   1 loaf rustic Italian bread
>   3 cloves garlic, peeled
>   Fresh sage leaves for garnish

In a large bowl gently blend cooked beans, balsamic vinegar, pepper, salt and olive oil. Take care not to break or mash beans. Slice bread, and toast in a 375°F oven until hard and browned to create crostini. Rub each crostini with garlic cloves. Cut crostini in half, and arrange on a large platter. Top each piece of bread with a generous portion of beans and more olive oil. Garnish platter with fresh sage, and serve as a first course or appetizer.

Add chicken stock to leftover beans to create a delicious soup.

Sour Cream Apple Pie

>   1 1/4 Cups sour cream
>   2 eggs
>   1 1/2 Cups sugar
>   2 1/4 teaspoons vanilla extract
>   1/3 teaspoon salt
>   2 Tablespoons all-purpose flour
>   2 pounds Granny Smith apples
>   1 dough recipe for a 9-inch pie
>   8 Tablespoons (1 stick) butter,
>   cut into thin pats
>   1 1/2 Cups Apple Pie Topping
>   (recipe follows)

Combine sour cream and eggs in large mixing bowl. Whip until creamy. Add sugar, vanilla, salt and flour. Blend thoroughly. Core and slice unpeeled apples directly into sour cream mixture. Stir to coat apples.

Use your fingers to press pie dough gently into 9-inch springform pan. Add sour cream apple mixture, and spread Apple Pie Topping evenly over filling. Top with butter pats. Bake in 350°F oven for 2 hours 20 minutes.

For Apple Pie Topping
>   1/2 Cup all-purpose flour
>   1/3 Cup brown sugar
>   1/2 Cup walnut pieces
>   1 Tablespoon cinnamon

Combine ingredients in food processor, and pulse until mixture is coarsely crumbled.

Jambalaya

STEVE DOMINICK
CHEF-PROPRIETOR

New Orleans Cookery in Chapel Hill serves up the fire and flair of Louisiana's French, Creole and Cajun culinary traditions. Under the able guidance of chef-owner Steve Dominick diners are treated to the earthy, spicy flavors that only the "Big Easy" and the bayou have the right to claim.

Fresh Vegetable and Herb Gumbo

For the Vegetable Stock
    2 quarts water
    1 onion stuck with 6 whole cloves
    2 ribs celery, coarsely chopped
    1 carrot, coarsely chopped
    1 teaspoon salt
    1 Cup tomato puree
    3 bay leaves
    6 black peppercorns
Combine all ingredients in a deep pot, and simmer for 45 minutes. Strain, and reserve liquid.

For the Gumbo
    1/4 Cup peanut oil
    1 Cup diced onion
    1 Cup diced celery
    1 Cup diced bell pepper
        (your choice of colors)
    3/4 Cup olive oil
    1 Cup all-purpose flour
    1 Cup cooked lima beans
    1 Cup cooked corn kernels
    2 Cups fresh okra, cut into 1/4-inch slices
    1 Cup diced fresh tomatoes
    2 Tablespoons gumbo file
    2 Tablespoons blackened seasoning
        [See *Cook's Notes & Glossary*]
    2 Tablespoons chopped fresh basil
    2 Tablespoons chopped fresh oregano
    2 Tablespoons chopped fresh tarragon
        (1 teaspoon dried)
    Salt and cayenne pepper to taste

Heat peanut oil in a large soup pot. Add onion, celery and bell peppers, and sauté approximately 10 minutes or until tender. Add vegetable stock, and bring to a boil.

Combine olive oil and flour in a small sauté pan. Whisk over medium-high heat until well combined and golden brown, approximately 4 minutes. Use a whisk to incorporate the golden roux into vegetable stock. Simmer for 20 minutes, stirring occasionally.

Add remaining ingredients, and simmer for 30 minutes. Serve over rice pilaf.

Jambalaya

2 Tablespoons olive oil
1 Tablespoon minced garlic
1/2 Cup diced yellow onion
1/2 Cup diced celery
1/2 Cup diced green bell pepper
1/2 Cup diced red bell pepper
1 chicken, bone in, cut into 8 pieces
2 Cups long-grain rice
6 Cups chicken stock
1 Cup tomato puree
4 bay leaves
2 teaspoons blackened seasoning
    [See *Cook's Notes & Glossary*]
1 teaspoon salt
1 teaspoon Tabasco® Sauce
1 teaspoon Italian seasoning
2 pounds Andouille sausage,
    cut into 2-inch pieces [See *Editor's Note*]
16 large shrimp, peeled and deveined

Heat oil in a large skillet over medium heat. Add garlic, onion, celery, red and green bell peppers, and sauté for 1 minute. Add chicken, and sauté until brown. Add rice, and stir to coat grains well. Add stock, tomato puree and all seasonings. Stir to mix completely. Cover, and bring to a boil. Immediately lower heat to a simmer, and cook for 15 minutes. Add sausage and shrimp. Stir once, then simmer for 5 more minutes or until rice is cooked. Let stand, covered, for 10 minutes, then serve.

Fried Catfish with Ravigote Sauce and Miniature Hushpuppies

For the Hushpuppies

1 Cup House Autry® Hushpuppy Mix
2 Tablespoons diced country ham
2 Tablespoons diced scallions

Prepare hushpuppy mix according to package instructions, adding ham and scallions to batter. Use a small mellon baller to make miniature hushpuppies. Fry in hot oil used to fry fish (see below), and set aside on paper towels to drain.

For the Fried Catfish

1 Cup milk
2 eggs
2 Cups all-purpose flour
1 teaspoon creole or blackened seasoning
    [See *Cook's Notes & Glossary*]
2 Cups corn flour or finely ground cornmeal
    [See *Editor's Note*]
1 pound farm-raised catfish,
    cut into 2-ounce pieces
4 Cups oil for frying

Heat oil in deep cast iron skillet to 350°F. Mix milk and eggs, and place in flat bowl or pie plate. Combine seasoning and all-purpose flour, and place on paper plate. Place finely ground corn-meal on paper plate. Dip catfish pieces first in seasoned flour, then in milk and egg mixture, and finally in corn flour. Place each piece on baking sheet until all pieces are breaded. Cook catfish pieces in hot oil until they float and are golden brown. Drain on paper towels.

For the Ravigote Sauce
>1/2 Cup mayonnaise
>1/2 Cup sour cream
>2 Tablespoons finely chopped dill pickles
>2 Tablespoons finely chopped capers
>1 hard-boiled egg, chopped
>Creole or blackened seasoning to taste
>1/4 Cup lemon juice
>Dash Tabasco® Sauce

Combine all ingredients and reserve.

To Assemble
>8 ounces bitter greens, such as endive,
>   chicory, mustard, etc.
>1 Tablespoon red wine vinegar
>3 Tablespoons pure olive oil

Mix vinegar and oil, and add greens. Toss to coat greens well. Portion greens evenly among 6 plates. Top each salad with fried catfish. Place a spoonful of Ravigote Sauce on edge of each plate, and arrange miniature hushpuppies around greens.

▼ ▼
White Chocolate Bread Pudding with Whiskey Crème Anglaise

>2 Cups cubed stale French bread
>1/3 Cup melted butter
>12 eggs
>2 Cups sugar
>1 Tablespoon ground cinnamon
>4 Cups milk, scalded
>2 Cups grated Baker's® white chocolate

Drizzle melted butter over bread cubes, and toast in oven until golden.

Beat eggs, cinnamon and sugar together by hand. Slowly add scalded milk while beating.

Place toasted bread cubes in a 9- by 13-inch pan. Scatter grated chocolate over cubes. Pour in custard, and bake in a water bath, in a 350°F oven for 40 to 45 minutes, or until center is barely firm when touched.

For the Whiskey Crème Anglaise
>2 Cups dark brown sugar
>8 Tablespoons (1 stick) butter
>1 Cup heavy cream
>4 Tablespoons bourbon or blended whiskey
>6 egg yolks
>1/4 teaspoon salt

Mix all ingredients in a small saucepan, and bring to a simmer, whisking continuously. Whisk for approximately 5 minutes until thickened. Keep warm until ready to serve.

Editor's Note
• *Andouille sausage is a highly spiced, smoked sausage. It can be purchased at Wellspring Groceries in Raleigh and Durham or Fowlers Gourmet in Durham.*
• *Corn flour or finely ground cornmeal can be made by placing regular cornmeal in a food processor, fitted with the metal blade, and processing until meal turns to flour.*

Galakitoboureko (Phyllo with Semolina Custard Filling)

Papas Grill

**KLEANTHIS
"PAPAS"
PAPANIKAS
CHEF-PROPRIETOR**

Papas Grill in Durham presents upscale Mediterranean cuisine as well as Greek family cookery with traditional recipes honed by chef-proprietor Kleanthis "Papas" Papanikas. Their twice-annual "Greek Night" celebrations feature a lavish Greek buffet, live music, traditional Greek dancing and, sometimes, a broken plate or two.

▼▼▼▼▼▼▼▼▼▼▼▼▼▼▼▼▼▼▼▼▼▼▼▼▼▼▼▼▼
Blue Crab Soup

3 3/4 Cups coarsely chopped onions
1 1/2 Cups coarsely chopped celery
1 Cup coarsely chopped carrots
1/4 Cup olive oil
6 blue crabs, cleaned [See *Editor's Note*]
1 teaspoon seafood seasoning
    [See *Editor's Note*]
1 Tablespoon chopped fresh rosemary
1 Tablespoon chopped fresh thyme
4 to 5 bay leaves
Salt and freshly ground black pepper
1/2 Cup dry white wine
1/2 Cup brandy
1/2 Cup dry sherry
3/4 Cup clam juice
2 Cups chicken stock
2 Cups water
5 teaspoons lemon juice
6 Tablespoons butter
6 Tablespoons all-purpose flour
2 Cups heavy cream
1/2 pound lump crab meat

Using a heavy, deep saucepan over high heat, sauté onions, celery and carrots in olive oil until vegetables are brown. Add cleaned crabs, simmer with vegetables for 5 minutes. Add seafood seasoning, herbs, spices, wine, brandy, and sherry. Bring to a boil, and boil for 3 minutes. Add chicken stock and water, stir well and cover. Simmer for 1 hour.

Melt butter in a small saucepan. Add flour, and whisk constantly to make a roux. When thick and creamy, remove from heat, and reserve.

Strain stock through a fine-mesh strainer into clean pot, pressing the solids to extract as much liquid as possible. Discard solids, including crabs. Take 1 cup of liquid and whisk it into reserved roux. Add roux back to pot of stock, and boil for 20 minutes. Add cream. Reduce heat, and simmer 5 minutes.

Place a portion of lump crab meat in the bottom of a soup bowl, and ladle hot soup over the crab. Serve immediately.

Taramasalata

5 slices white bread
3 1/2 ounces tarama (orange carp fish roe)
1/2 Cup finely chopped onions
1/2 Cup olive oil
1 1/2 Cups lemon juice
Olives and chopped fresh parsley
    for garnish

Remove crust from bread. Put bread in bowl, and add enough water to barely cover bread. Soak for approximately 3 minutes. Squeeze bread to remove as much water as possible.

Place bread in food processor. Add fish roe and onions, and pulse on and off until smooth. Add olive oil and lemon juice while processor is running. Transfer to serving bowl, and garnish with olives and parsley.

Beef Tenderloin and Penne Pasta

1 1/2 pounds beef tenderloin, cubed
Salt and freshly ground black pepper
1/4 Cup olive oil
1/2 Cup chopped scallions
1/2 Cup diced red bell pepper
1/2 Cup diced mushrooms
1 Tablespoon minced garlic
3 Tablespoons balsamic vinegar
1/2 Cup peeled, seeded and diced tomatoes
3 Tablespoons red wine
1 1/2 Cups tomato sauce
3 Tablespoons feta cheese
1 pound (dry weight) penne pasta cooked
    according to package directions

Heat large skillet over high heat. Season beef with salt and pepper. When skillet is hot add oil, then beef. Toss beef to lightly cook cubes on all sides, about 2 minutes. Add vegetables and garlic, and mix well. Add vinegar, tomatoes and red wine. Mix thoroughly. Add tomato sauce, feta cheese and cooked pasta. Simmer for 2 minutes. Adjust seasonings to taste. Serve immediately.

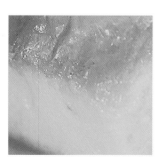

Fish in Phyllo Dough

For Each Portion

1 grouper or wahoo fillet (8-ounces)
3 sheets phyllo dough
1/2 Cup melted butter
2 1/4-inch vertical slices grilled zucchini
1 small grilled red bell pepper
1 artichoke heart (canned or frozen)

Grill the fish lightly until grill marks are light brown. Place one sheet of phyllo on a baking sheet, and brush with melted butter. Fold in half horizontally, and brush top with butter. Top with a second sheet of phyllo, and follow same directions for the first.

When you have 6 layers, and the top layer is buttered, place grilled fish fillet in middle of pastry. Stack the zucchini, red bell pepper and artichoke heart on top of fish. Completely enclose in phyllo by wrapping pastry up and over the fish and vegetables. Brush outside of phyllo with butter, and bake in a 375°F oven for 20 minutes.

Galakitoboureko

(Phyllo with Semolina Custard Filling)

4 Cups cold milk
3/4 Cup semolina flour
5 eggs
1 Cup sugar
1 Cup melted butter, divided
1 teaspoon lemon zest
16 sheets phyllo dough

Place milk in a deep saucepan. Whisking constantly to avoid lumps, add semolina to milk. Bring mixture to boil, stirring constantly, and boil for 1 minute. Remove from heat, and cool for 5 minutes. In a separate bowl beat eggs and sugar together until fluffy, about 4 minutes. Add to semolina mixture, then add 1/2 cup melted butter and lemon zest, and blend well.

Brush 8 phyllo sheets with melted butter and layer in a buttered 13- by 9-inch baking pan. Allow phyllo to extend up sides of pan. Spread filling evenly over pastry. Fold sides and ends of phyllo over filling. Trim 8 more pieces of pastry to fit inside baking dish. Brush each with melted butter, and place on top of filling. Use a sharp knife to cut top layer of pastry only into 4 equal rows. Do not cut through filling. Bake at 350°F for 45 minutes. Remove from oven, and drizzle with cold syrup. Return to oven for 5 minutes. Remove, and let stand 2 hours before serving. To serve cut into diamonds or squares. Refrigerate leftovers.

For the Syrup

2 1/2 Cups sugar
1 1/2 Cups water
3 thin slices lemon
1 cinnamon stick

Combine all ingredients in a saucepan, and bring to a boil. Reduce heat, and simmer for 10 minutes. Allow to cool completely. Remove lemon and cinnamon before using.

Editor's Note
• *Blue crabs may be unavailable for the soup. If so, use 2 pounds of snow crab legs. In either case, leave the shells intact as they create an intense crab flavor.*
• *Seafood seasoning is easy to make. Place at least 1 tablespoon of Crab and Shrimp Boil (any brand will do) in a food processor or spice grinder. Process to a fine powder. Store in an airtight container.*

Carrot Ginger Soup

Chicken Breast Stuffed with Lobster-Fried-Caper Mousse

Yellow Tomato, Sugared Beet and Toasted Almond Goat Cheese Buttons

ANDREW BOOGER
CHEF-PROPRIETOR

Portobello Restaurant is a contemporary eatery where Chef Andrew Booger's stone-fired pizzas are the talk of the neighborhood, as are his eclectic entrees. His loyal patrons enjoy the intimate atmosphere and inventive menu in this popular North Raleigh restaurant.

Carrot Ginger Soup

4 Tablespoons butter
4 large carrots, peeled
2 Tablespoons diced fresh ginger
Salt and freshly ground black pepper
2 quarts chicken stock

For the Garnish
6 large shiitake mushroom caps
1 teaspoon fresh thyme
1 Tablespoon olive oil
Salt and freshly ground black pepper

In a 4-quart soup pot over medium heat melt butter. Add carrots, and turn up heat to medium-high. Sauté carrots for 5 minutes, then add chopped ginger. Reduce heat to medium, and season with salt and pepper. Add stock, and bring soup to a simmer. Cook for 30 to 45 minutes or until carrots are tender. Use a blender to puree soup. Reserve.

While soup is cooking marinate mushrooms in thyme, olive oil, salt and pepper. Grill mushrooms over medium-hot charcoal fire until tender.

To serve, ladle soup into soup plates, and place one mushroom cap in center of each bowl.

Yellow Tomato, Sugared Beet and Toasted Almond Goat Cheese Buttons

2 large beets
1/4 Cup champagne vinegar
2 Tablespoons sugar
Salt and freshly ground black pepper
1 Cup toasted sliced almonds
12-ounce goat cheese log, cut into
   6 equal slices
2 heads frisée (curly endive)
Balsamic vinegar
Olive oil
6 medium-size yellow tomatoes

Wash beets, and remove tops 1 inch above the bulb. Place beets on a baking sheet, and roast in a 350°F oven for 1 hour or until beets are soft when pricked with a fork. Cool, trim the ends, and peel away the skin. Cut beets into quarters, then slice into triangles about 1/6-inch thick. Put beets in a bowl and toss with sugar, vinegar and salt and pepper. Refrigerate for at least 8 hours.

Toast sliced almonds in a 350°F oven for 3 to 5 minutes or until lightly brown. Use a food processor fitted with the steel blade and coarsely chop nuts. Coat each slice of goat cheese with chopped almonds. Bake breaded goat cheese slices in 350°F oven for 3 minutes or until warmed through.

Remove root end of frisée, and wash thoroughly. Toss frisée in 1 part balsamic vinegar and 3 parts olive oil. Place a handful of dressed greens on each plate. Top each portion with a sliced yellow tomato, then sugared beets, then baked goat cheese, and garnish with remaining crumbled almonds and a splash of balsamic vinegar.

Pan-Seared Filet Mignon with Pinot Noir Shallot Sauce

6 filet mignons (7-ounces each)
1 Tablespoon olive oil
1/2 Cup sliced shallots
2 pounds fresh black trumpet mushrooms,
   cleaned, stems removed
1 1/2 teaspoons chopped fresh thyme
2 Cups Pinot Noir
Salt and freshly ground black pepper

Using a heavy-bottom, non-reactive skillet sear meat over high heat. When steaks are brown on both sides transfer them to a baking sheet. Place meat in a 350°F oven for 6 to 8 minutes or until desired doneness.

Return skillet to medium-high heat, and add olive oil. When hot add shallots, and cook until translucent. Add mushrooms, thyme, salt and pepper, and cook for 3 minutes. Add wine, and raise heat to high. Cook until liquid is reduced by half. Season with salt and pepper to taste.

Arrange mushrooms equally on 6 plates. Top with a filet mignon and spoon sauce over presentation. Serve immediately.

Chicken Breast Stuffed with Lobster-Fried-Caper Mousse

2 live lobsters (1 1/4-pounds each)
1 Cup water
1 1/2 Cup wine, divided
Salt
White pepper
1/2 Cup heavy cream
3 Tablespoons vegetable oil
3 Tablespoons capers
6 whole chicken breasts, skinned,
     trimmed and pounded to even thickness

Steam lobsters in white wine and water for 7 to 10 minutes. Cool.

When lobster meat has cooled remove from shell, and place in food processor with salt and white pepper to taste. Process by pulsing on and off until almost pureed. With processor running continuously add cream in a slow, steady stream. Remove, and reserve.

Drain capers, and pat dry with paper towels. Heat vegetable oil in a small skillet, and fry capers 1 minute. Drain, and cool. Mix capers into lobster mousse by hand. Refrigerate for 45 minutes.

Place chicken breast skin side down in palm of your hand. Scoop approximately 2 tablespoons mousse into center of breast, and fold chicken around mousse until it resembles a baseball, and all mousse is sealed inside the chicken. Continue until all breasts are stuffed. Place breasts on baking pan, surround with remaining wine, and bake in a 350°F oven for 30 to 45 minutes until tender. Slice breasts, and arrange in a fan pattern on each plate.

White Chocolate Banana Mousse Pie

This recipe is courtesy of Marget and Frank Ballard of Carolina Cakery. Carolina Cakery prepares most of the desserts for Portobello Restaurant.

1 prepared graham cracker crust
2 1/2 Cups sugar
1 Cup water
6 egg yolks
3 Tablespoons butter
4 ounces Baker's® white chocolate, melted
1 Cup heavy cream, whipped
3 ripe bananas
Shaved dark chocolate for garnish (optional)

Combine sugar and water in a saucepan over medium heat, and cook until sugar is completely dissolved. Increase heat to high, and boil for 5 minutes. Using an electric mixer on high speed beat egg yolks for 2 minutes. Reduce speed to low and, add sugar water. Mix 15 minutes increasing mixer speed every few minutes. After 15 minutes reduce speed to low, and add butter. Blend until smooth. Add melted white chocolate, and blend until smooth. Gently fold in whipped cream.

Line bottom of crust with 1 banana sliced into thin rounds. Add one quarter of mousse, and repeat layering until all bananas and mousse are used, ending with mousse. Refrigerate 2 hours before serving. Garnish with shaved dark chocolate if desired.

Pyewacket Restaurant in Chapel Hill is a feast of international flavors, from Italy to the American Southwest. Chef Robert Cates takes great pride in dishing up his inventive cuisine to both the local university crowd and visiting VIPs. Don't be fooled, there are some serious tastes in this whimsically named restaurant.

Lime Sour Cream Pie

ROBERT "MUSKIE" CATES CHEF

Gnocchi with Two Sauces

For the Gnocchi

        1 Tablespoon butter
        8 ounces frozen chopped spinach,
            thawed and squeezed dry
        3 Cups cooked and riced Idaho potatoes
            (approximately 2 potatoes)
        3 Tablespoons basil pesto
        1 egg
        1/4 teaspoon salt
        1/8 teaspoon freshly ground black pepper
        3/4 Cup all-purpose flour

In a small skillet over medium heat melt butter, add spinach, and cook until completely dry. Remove spinach from heat, and cool. Mix spinach with potatoes, pesto, egg, salt and pepper. Gradually add flour.

Knead to form a soft dough, about 5 minutes. Try not to overwork dough or it will become sticky.

Scatter a scant handful of flour onto a clean flat surface. Take a handful of dough and roll it into finger-width ropes. Place ropes on a small tray covered with parchment or waxed paper, and freeze for 10 minutes. Cut ropes into 1-inch pieces. Gnocchi can be made ahead and stored in freezer until ready to cook.

For the Cheese Sauce

        3 Tablespoons butter
        2 teaspoons minced garlic
        1 1/2 Tablespoons minced shallots
        3/4 Cup white wine
        2 Tablespoons crumbled Gorgonzola cheese
        1/2 Cup half-and-half
        1/2 Cup heavy cream
        2 Tablespoons grated Parmesan cheese

Heat butter in a non-stick skillet over medium heat. Add garlic and shallots, and sauté for 2 minutes. Add wine, and reduce to 1/3 cup liquid. Add Gorgonzola, and stir to melt. Add both creams, and bring to a simmer. Stir in Parmesan cheese, and cook on low for 15 minutes. Remove sauce from heat, and keep warm.

Chicken and Clove Soup

        5 Cups chicken stock
        7 whole cloves
        2 Cups white wine
        1 Tablespoon salt
        1 1/2 teaspoons oregano
        1 1/2 teaspoons freshly ground black pepper
        2 cans (14 1/2-ounces each) chopped tomatoes
        1 Cup cut green beans (1/2-inch long),
            tips removed
        1 Cup diced celery
        2/3 Cup diced onion
        4 Cups peeled, diced potatoes
        1 1/2 Cups frozen green peas
        2 Cups cooked chicken, cut into
            bite-size pieces

Boil chicken stock, cloves and wine in a soup pot for 5 minutes. Add salt, oregano, pepper, tomatoes, beans, celery and onions. Cook for 15 minutes, then add potatoes. Cook until potatoes are tender, then add peas. Cook for 5 minutes more, and add chicken. Cook for 1 to 2 minutes to thoroughly heat chicken, and serve.

For the Rosemary Sauce

    1/4 Cup olive oil
    1 teaspoon minced garlic
    1/3 Cup minced shallots
    2 teaspoons chopped fresh basil
    1 teaspoon salt
    1 teaspoon freshly ground black pepper
    1/2 teaspoon chopped fresh thyme
    2 cans chopped tomatoes (28-ounces each),
       drained
    2 teaspoons red wine vinegar
    2 teaspoons balsamic vinegar
    2 teaspoons chopped fresh rosemary

Heat a sauté pan over medium-high heat, and add olive oil. When oil is hot add garlic, shallots, basil, salt, pepper and thyme. Sauté for 3 minutes. Add tomatoes and vinegars, and simmer for 30 minutes, stirring often. Be careful not to burn sauce.

Remove pan from heat and stir in rosemary. Puree 2 cups of sauce in a food processor or blender. Reserve.

To Assemble

Bring 1 gallon of water to a boil. Add 2 teaspoons salt and remove gnocchi from freezer as needed. Use 10 gnocchi per person. Drop gnocchi into boiling water 20 to 30 at a time. Wait until water returns to a boil before adding more. When gnocchi float to the surface wait 45 seconds, then remove with a slotted spoon, and spread out on a bed of paper towels to drain.

Preheat oven to 400°F. Using small oven-proof plates, place 10 gnocchi in a circle on each plate. Spread 4 tablespoons pureed rosemary sauce over half of each plate, covering 5 gnocchi. Spread 1 tablespoon cheese sauce over other 5 gnocchi. Sprinkle 1 tablespoon of Parmesan over top of each presentation, and bake for 5 to 6 minutes. Plates may be prepared ahead and heated just before serving.

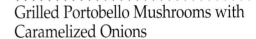

Grilled Portobello Mushrooms with Caramelized Onions

For the Portobello Mushrooms

    1/2 Cup olive oil
    1 Tablespoon minced garlic
    6 large portobello mushroom caps
    Chopped fresh parsley for garnish

Combine oil and garlic, and brush mushroom caps on both sides with mixture. Grill mushrooms 3 to 4 minutes on each side. Reserve.

For the Caramelized Onions

    3 Tablespoons butter
    8 large yellow onions, peeled and sliced
    1 Tablespoon salt
    2 teaspoons freshly ground black pepper

Melt butter in a large sauté pan, and add sliced onions. Cook over low heat for 40 to 45 minutes or until onions are golden brown and beginning to caramelize. Add salt and pepper, and keep warm.

For the Vinaigrette

    1 teaspoon sugar
    1 1/2 teaspoons salt
    1 1/2 teaspoons freshly ground black pepper
    1 teaspoon minced garlic
    1/4 Cup champagne vinegar
    1/2 Cup balsamic vinegar
    1 Tablespoon lemon juice
    1 Cup peanut oil
    1/2 Cup walnut oil

Place all ingredients except oils in blender, and blend on medium speed for 1 minute. With blender running add oils in a slow, steady stream until vinaigrette thickens. Reserve.

For the Mashed Potatoes

    4 large or 6 medium-size potatoes
    1/2 Cup half-and-half
    4 Tablespoons butter

Boil potatoes until tender, and mash with cream and butter. Keep in a covered metal bowl placed over hot water.

To Assemble

Place a mound of mashed potatoes in center of each plate. Slice each mushroom cap in quarters, and place across each portion of potatoes. Spoon hot onions and vinaigrette in a band across each mushroom. Garnish with chopped fresh parsley, if desired.

Baked Snapper Achiote

For the Achiote Sauce
>3 Tablespoons annatto seeds
> [See *Editor's Note*]
>2 Cups boiling water
>1/3 Cup orange juice
>1/4 Cup cider vinegar
>2 teaspoons minced garlic
>1/2 teaspoon minced dried ancho chili
> pepper, soaked to soften, and de-seeded
>1 teaspoon ground cumin
>1 teaspoon ground allspice
>1/2 teaspoon salt
>1/4 teaspoon freshly ground black pepper
>1 teaspoon sugar
>1 Tablespoon chopped orange zest (1 orange)
>1/4 Cup peanut or soy oil

Cover annatto seeds with boiling water, and let sit, covered, for 8 hours. Drain annatto seeds, and place all ingredients in blender. Blend on medium-high speed for 40 seconds. Reserve.

For the Orange Cream Sauce
>1 Cup low fat yogurt, drained for
> at least 30 minutes
>1 Cup sour cream
>3 Tablespoons orange juice concentrate

Mix strained yogurt with sour cream and orange juice concentrate. Reserve.

To Prepare the Snapper
>6 snapper fillets (8-ounces each),
> boned and trimmed
>1/2 Cup thinly sliced scallions
>3 Cups cooked white rice
>6 thin fresh orange slices for garnish

Place snapper fillets on a lightly oiled baking sheet. Cover each fillet with 2 tablespoons achiote sauce. Bake in a 400°F oven for 8 to 10 minutes or until firm, and flesh is opaque throughout. Serve snapper on bed of white rice, and sprinkle with scallions. Top each piece of fish with 1 heaping tablespoon of orange cream sauce, and garnish with a thin orange slice.

Lime Sour Cream Pie

For the Crust
>1 Cup graham cracker crumbs
>2 Tablespoons sugar
>1/4 teaspoon ground ginger
>2 Tablespoons melted butter

Combine ingredients in a bowl, and mix well. Press mixture evenly into a 9-inch pie plate, and bake at 325°F for 9 minutes. Remove from oven, and cool completely.

For the Filling
>2/3 Cup sugar
>1/4 Cup cornstarch
>1/2 Cup fresh lime juice
>1 Cup half-and-half
>1 Tablespoon butter
>1/4 teaspoon salt
>2/3 Cup sour cream
>4 teaspoons lime zest

Mix sugar, cornstarch and salt in top of double boiler. Add lime juice, and whisk to combine well.

Scald half-and-half in microwave on high for 1 minute. Add cream, butter and salt to lime mixture, and blend well. Cover, and cook, stirring occasionally, until mixture is thick and translucent. Pour onto metal baking sheet with sides, and let cool at least 30 minutes. Cut cooled mixture into rough chunks, and place in food processor. Add sour cream and lime zest. Pulse until well combined.

Pour mixture into cooled crust, and spread evenly. Top with whipped cream, and garnish with thin lime wheels.

For the Topping
>1 Cup heavy cream
>4 teaspoons sugar
>2 thinly sliced limes

Whip cream with sugar until soft peaks form. Use lime slices for garnish.

Editor's Note
• *Annatto comes from achiote seed, however the two terms are often used interchangeably. Seeds should be a rusty red color. Ones that have turned brown are old and flavorless. The seeds impart a slightly musky flavor and have no substitution. You can buy annatto at Wellspring.*

JIM GROOT
PROPRIETOR

Red Hot & Blue is a "Memphis-style" barbecue restaurant with locations in Raleigh, Cary and Chapel Hill. Publications, including the Washington Post *and* Conde Nast's Traveler *have lavished praise on the food, service and atmosphere. A customer, whose name no one remembered to ask, was heard to say, "Best barbecue I ever had in a building that hadn't already been condemned."*

Smoked Brisket Chili

1 1/2 pounds smoked beef brisket,
   cubed (recipe below)
2 teaspoons butter
1 1/2 Cups coarsely chopped onion
1/2 teaspoon minced jalapeño pepper
2 cans roma tomatoes (28-ounces each)
   with juice
1 teaspoon freshly ground black pepper
1 Tablespoon chili powder
1 Tablespoon ground cumin
1/2 teaspoon cayenne pepper
1 pound dark kidney beans, cooked

To Smoke Brisket

Rub 3-pound beef brisket with salt and pepper, and smoke in home smoker using low heat for about 6 hours.

For the Chili

Melt butter in a large sauté pan. Add onions and jalapeño, and sauté for 5 minutes. Add tomatoes, cumin, chili powder, cayenne and black pepper. Mix thoroughly. Cut smoked brisket into 3/4-inch cubes, and add to tomato mixture. Cover, and simmer for 20 minutes. Uncover, add kidney beans, and heat through. Serve.

Corn Relish

1 pound fresh or frozen corn kernels
3/4 Cup diced green bell pepper
1/2 Cup diced red bell pepper
1/2 Cup diced red onion
1 teaspoon diced jalapeño pepper
1/4 Cup coarsely chopped cilantro leaves
1/2 Cup T. Marzetti's Whalers Wharf® dressing [See *Editor's Note*]
12 tomato slices

Combine all ingredients, except tomato. Chill, and serve on sliced tomatoes.

Smoked Turkey Breast with Spicy Honey Mustard

About Smoking Turkey

Use a 6- to 8-pound turkey breast and a home smoker or kettle grill. Hickory chips impart a delicious flavor, but pecan chips, mesquite and other woods can be used as well. Soak chips in water for 30 minutes before adding to smoker or grill.

Smoke turkey at 175°F for about 5 hours. The internal temperature should reach 160°F. Remove meat from smoker, and let turkey rest for at least 20 minutes before carving.

For the Sauce

1 Cup honey
2 Cups Dijon mustard
1 Cup mayonnaise
1/3 Cup red wine vinegar
1/3 Cup Tabasco® Sauce
1 teaspoon freshly ground black pepper

Mix all ingredients, and blend until smooth. Thin with honey or thicken with mayonnaise until sauce pours easily, but is not too runny.

To Serve

Slice turkey with the grain into 3/4-inch thick slices. Place slices on each plate, and ladle 1/4 cup of Spicy Honey Mustard Sauce over turkey.

Peanut Butter Pie

3/4 Cup unsweetened peanut butter
8-ounce package cream cheese, softened
1 Cup light brown sugar
2 teaspoons vanilla extract
3/4 Cup heavy cream
1 8-inch baked pie crust (crumb crust
    may be used)

Blend peanut butter, cream cheese and brown sugar until smooth. Add vanilla and cream, and stir with a whisk. Do not whip or beat at fast speed.

Pour filling into pie crust, and refrigerate for at least 12 hours.

Editor's Note
• Whalers Wharf® dressing is made by T. Marzetti, and is available at Hannaford's.

Vegetarian Lasagna

Simple Pleasures
Market & Cafe

BATES PLUMMER
KITCHEN MANAGER
AND
TODD O'BRIEN
HEAD COOK

Part gourmet market, part beautiful gift ware for the home, and part cafe, Simple Pleasures lives up to its name for the sophisticated clientele that frequent this Old Raleigh specialty shop.

▼▼▼▼▼▼▼▼▼▼▼▼▼▼▼▼▼▼▼▼▼▼▼▼▼▼▼▼▼▼▼▼
Salmon Benedict

1 teaspoon butter
1/2 Cup diced red bell pepper,
    plus extra for garnish
1/3 Cup diced scallions,
    plus extra for garnish
1/2 Cup diced celery
1/4 teaspoon minced garlic
1 egg, beaten
1/3 Cup mayonnaise
1 Tablespoon Dijon mustard
2 teaspoons Worcestershire sauce
1/2 teaspoon Tabasco® Sauce
1/2 teaspoon dried dill
1 Tablespoon salt
1 teaspoon freshly ground black pepper
1 1/2 pounds salmon, poached,
    skinned and flaked
2 Cups fresh breadcrumbs
2 Tablespoons butter
1 Tablespoon peanut oil

Melt butter in sauté pan over medium-high heat, and add red bell peppers, scallions, celery and garlic. Sauté 4 to 5 minutes or until tender. Set aside.

Use fork to mix egg, mayonnaise, mustard, Worcestershire, Tabasco, dill, salt and pepper until well blended. Add sautéed vegetables, and combine. Gently fold in flaked salmon and breadcrumbs. Chill for 2 hours.

Divide salmon mixture into 6 portions and make uniform patties.

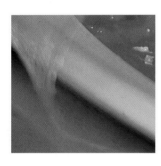

Melt butter, and combine with peanut oil in skillet over medium-high heat. When oil is hot cook patties until well browned on both sides. Be careful not to crowd them in pan. Drain patties on paper towels, and keep warm.

To Assemble
> 6 slices sourdough or any substantial bread, toasted
> 6 poached eggs
> Hollandaise sauce
> [See *Cook's Notes & Glossary*]

Top each slice toast with salmon patty, then with poached egg, and finally with hollandaise sauce. Garnish with chopped red bell pepper and scallion if desired.

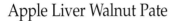

Apple Liver Walnut Pate

For the Chicken Livers
> 2 Tablespoons butter
> 1 pound chicken livers, rinsed and dried
> 12 ounces Neese's® hot sausage

Melt butter in sauté pan over medium-high heat, and sauté livers and sausage until cooked but not brown. Do not overcook. Drain, and discard fat.

For the Pate
> 8 Tablespoons (1 stick) butter
> 3 1/2 Cups peeled, cored and chopped Granny Smith apples
> 2 Cups chopped yellow onion
> 3 teaspoons chopped garlic
> 3/4 Cup chopped shallots
> 1 pound cream cheese, room temperature
> 1 2/3 Cups walnut pieces
> 1/2 teaspoon ground allspice
> 1 teaspoon dried tarragon
> 1 teaspoon dried thyme
> 2 teaspoons salt
> 1/2 teaspoon freshly ground black pepper

Melt butter in large skillet over medium heat. Add apples, onion, garlic and shallots, and cook until all moisture is evaporated. Reserve.

Blend meat and apple mixtures in a large bowl. Add cream cheese and walnut pieces, and mix thoroughly. Add herbs and spices, and puree mixture in food processor in small batches if necessary. Chill thoroughly before serving. This pate freezes well. Defrost in the refrigerator for 24 hours before bringing to room temperature, and serving.

Basil Chicken Salad

For the Chicken
> 2 pounds boneless, skinless chicken breasts
> 1/2 Cup olive oil
> 1/4 Cup balsamic vinegar
> 1 1/2 teaspoons minced garlic
> 2 teaspoons dried basil
> Salt and freshly ground black pepper
> Cherry tomatoes and red onion rings for garnish (optional)

Cut chicken into 1-inch strips. Combine remaining ingredients, except for garnish, and pour over chicken. Toss to coat completely. Marinate 6 to 8 hours in refrigerator. Before cooking drain, and discard marinade. Heat a non-stick skillet over medium-high heat. When hot add chicken, and cook until browned on all sides. (Oil from the marinade will cling to chicken making additional oil unnecessary.) Keep warm in 250°F oven.

For the Vinaigrette
> 2 teaspoons Dijon mustard
> 1/2 teaspoon minced garlic
> 2 Tablespoons red wine vinegar
> 1/4 Cup olive oil
> 1/2 teaspoon ground cumin
> 2 Tablespoons dried basil
> 1 3/4 Cups peeled, seeded and finely diced tomatoes
> 1/4 Cup finely chopped red onion
> Salt and freshly ground black pepper

Combine ingredients, and mix well.

To Assemble
Place handful of mixed greens on each plate. Top with warm chicken, and pour vinaigrette over all. Garnish with cherry tomatoes and thinly sliced red onion rings if desired.

Vegetarian Lasagna

2 1/2 pounds cottage cheese
4 eggs, beaten
1 Cup grated Parmesan cheese
2 teaspoons dried basil
1 teaspoon freshly ground black pepper
1 Tablespoon olive oil
2 Cups sliced carrots
2 Cups sliced mushrooms
1 1/2 Cups sliced zucchini
4 Cups commercial marinara sauce
　(or make your own)
1 pound dry lasagna noodles
1 1/2 pounds frozen, chopped spinach,
　thawed and squeezed dry
1 pound mozzarella cheese, sliced
Grated Parmesan and chopped parsley
　for garnish

Mix cottage cheese, eggs, Parmesan, basil and black pepper together. Reserve.

In a skillet over medium-high heat add olive oil, carrots, mushrooms and zucchini, and sauté until *al dente*.

Cover bottom of 8 1/2- by 11-inch casserole with one third of marinara sauce. Add one layer of uncooked, dry lasagna noodles covering entire bottom of dish. Top with half of cottage cheese mixture, all spinach, half of the mozzarella, and the second third of the marinara sauce. Add another layer uncooked, dried lasagna noodles, remainder of cottage cheese mixture, all the vegetable mixture, remainder of lasagna noodles, remainder of marinara sauce and remainder of mozzarella.

Cover casserole first with plastic wrap, then with heavy-duty aluminum foil, completely sealing the casserole. Bake in a 350°F oven for 1 1/2 hours. Remove from oven, uncover pan, taking care to avoid steam. Top with grated Parmesan and chopped parsley. Allow to cool for 15 minutes before slicing.

Bread Pudding with Whiskey Sauce

9 Cups cubed French bread
1 quart milk
2 Cups sugar
4 eggs, beaten
1 Tablespoon vanilla extract

Pour milk over bread cubes, and let soak for 30 minutes. Whisk remaining ingredients for 2 minutes until well combined, and add to bread mixture. Pour into well-buttered 9- by 13-inch pan. Cover with foil, and bake at 325°F for 1 1/2 hours. Let cool completely, and serve with Whiskey Sauce.

For Whiskey Sauce

8 Tablespoons (1 stick) butter
1 Cup powdered (10X) sugar
1 egg, beaten
1/4 Cup whiskey

In a saucepan over medium heat, melt butter, and stir in powdered sugar. Reduce heat, and simmer for 2 minutes, stirring to dissolve sugar. Remove from heat, and quickly stir in beaten egg. Whisk until well combined. Add whiskey, and stir to combine. Cool sauce for 5 to 10 minutes. Serve warm.

Salmon in Puff Pastry with Champagne Sauce

Simpson's
Beef & Seafood Restaurant

SCOTT WATERS
EXECUTIVE CHEF

Simpson's in North Raleigh is known for its

upscale comfort and excellent service. In

cooler weather patrons gather by the fireplace

in the bar, whetting their appetites for

proprietor Mel Simpson's famous prime rib.

▼▼▼▼▼▼▼▼▼▼▼▼▼▼▼▼▼▼▼▼▼▼▼▼▼▼▼▼
Salmon in Puff Pastry with Champagne Sauce

6 salmon fillets (6-ounces each)
6 sheets of puff pastry (10- by 10-inches)
3 Cups cooked fresh spinach, squeezed dry
1/4 Cup finely chopped shallots
1/2 Cup clam juice
1 1/2 Cups champagne
2 Cups heavy cream
Chopped parsley for garnish (optional)

Unfold 1 piece of pastry, place 1 salmon fillet in middle, and top with 1/2 cup spinach. Fold dough to completely enclose salmon and spinach, and pinch edges to seal. Repeat procedure with remaining fillets. Place each wrapped fillet seam side down on baking sheet, and bake at 350°F for 20 minutes or until pastry is golden brown.

While salmon is baking combine shallots, clam juice and champagne. Boil until 1/3 cup of liquid remains. Strain, discard solids, and add heavy cream to remaining liquid. Reduce by one third.

To serve place 1 pastry package on each of 6 plates, and nap with sauce. Garnish with parsley if desired.

Shrimp Chez Simpson's

1/4 Cup butter
3/4 Cup chopped onion
3/4 Cup chopped mushrooms
1/2 Cup chopped red bell pepper
1/3 Cup dry sherry
1 teaspoon minced garlic
36 medium-size shrimp,
    shelled and deveined
1 head leaf lettuce

Melt butter in large sauté pan over medium heat. Add onions, mushrooms and red bell peppers, and cook for 4 minutes or until tender. Add sherry and garlic, and cook for 2 minutes. Add shrimp, and cook until they turn pink.

Line 6 individual plates with lettuce. Use tongs to arrange shrimp and vegetables on lettuce. Pour remaining juice from sautéing shrimp over top, and serve immediately.

Cabernet Sauvignon Sauce

2 Tablespoons olive oil
1/4 Cup finely chopped shallots
1 Tablespoon minced garlic
2 Tablespoons all-purpose flour
2 Cups full-bodied Cabernet Sauvignon
2 Tablespoons Dijon mustard
3 Tablespoons olive oil
Salt and freshly ground black pepper
1 Cup heavy cream
1 Tablespoon chopped fresh tarragon
    (optional)

In a 2-quart saucepan over high heat sauté shallots in olive oil until translucent. Add garlic, and cook for 30 seconds. Add flour, and mix to make a roux. Add wine, and bring to a boil. Reduce heat, and simmer until liquid is thickened and reduced by half. Whisk in mustard and cream, and cook for 1 minute. Taste and adjust seasonings if necessary. Add tarragon if desired.

Transfer sauce to a glass bowl, and refrigerate for 24 hours. To serve, bring to room temperature. Serve on grilled salmon or steak.

Chocolate Marquis

6 Tablespoons butter
1 pound semisweet chocolate,
    coarsely chopped
4 eggs, room temperature
1/4 Cup sugar
2 Cups heavy cream, whipped with 1
    Tablespoon sugar for garnish

Combine and melt butter and chocolate in top of a double boiler. Using an electric mixer on medium-high speed beat eggs and sugar until double in volume, approximately 10 minutes. Remove chocolate and butter from heat, and gradually add egg mixture, beating constantly to combine. Spoon mixture into 5-ounce ramekins until three quarters full. Place ramekins in a baking pan that has at least 1 1/2-inch slides. Pour boiling water into baking pan, taking care not to splash water into chocolate mixture. Place pan in 300°F oven, and bake for 1 1/2 hours. Serve Marquis with whipped cream.

Balsamic Chicken

Seared Tuna with Warm Napa Slaw

Grilled Pork with Port-Infused Onions

The Charter Room
at The Velvet Cloak Inn

JEFFERY HADLEY
EXECUTIVE CHEF

One of Raleigh's early upscale restaurants,

The Charter Room at The Velvet Cloak Inn

is still pleasing customers with their

Continental menu.

Three-Onion Soup

6 Tablespoons butter
1 leek, white part only, julienned
2 Cups sliced and quartered Vidalia onions
2 Cups sliced and quartered Bermuda onions
1 teaspoon minced garlic
1 teaspoon paprika
1/3 Cup all-purpose flour
12 ounces flat beer
1 Tablespoon chopped fresh marjoram
4 Cups beef stock
Salt and freshly ground black pepper
1 Cup half-and-half

Melt butter in a heavy-bottom saucepan. Add leeks, onions, garlic and paprika, and cook over medium-low heat until onions are translucent. Sprinkle flour over onions, and cook for 3 minutes, stirring constantly. Deglaze pan with beer, scraping brown bits from bottom of the pan. Add marjoram and beef stock, and bring to a simmer. Add salt and pepper to taste, and cook continue to cook on simmer for 15 minutes. Add cream, and cook for 1 minute. Soup can be refrigerated for up to 3 days.

Seared Tuna with Warm Napa Slaw

6 tuna medallions (3-ounces each)
1 teaspoon peanut oil

Heat oil in cast iron skillet until it begins to smoke. Place tuna medallions carefully in pan. Do not move them for 30 seconds to 1 minute. Turn medallions over, and sear for 30 seconds. Remove immediately from pan. Reserve.

For the Slaw

1 Cup julienned onion
3 Tablespoons olive oil
1 head napa cabbage, shredded
1/2 Cup white wine vinegar
1 Tablespoon celery salt
Salt and freshly ground black pepper
1/4 Cup sugar
4 ounces smoked shrimp [See *Editor's Note*]

Sauté onion in oil until softened, approximately 2 minutes. Add cabbage, and toss until wilted. Deglaze pan with vinegar, and add celery salt, salt, pepper and sugar. Mince half the smoked shrimp, and add to slaw, reserving remainder for garnish.

To Assemble

Portion warm slaw onto 6 individual plates, and top each with tuna medallion. Drizzle remaining juices from slaw over tuna. Garnish with remaining shrimp and chopped parsley if desired.

Balsamic Chicken

1 1/2 pounds skinless, boneless
    chicken breasts
1 teaspoon salt, plus extra to taste
1 teaspoon freshly ground black pepper,
    plus extra to taste
2/3 Cup olive oil, divided
1/3 Cup julienned sun-dried tomatoes
1 1/2 Cups diced shiitake mushrooms
1/4 Cup balsamic vinegar
2 Cups chicken stock
2 teaspoons crushed garlic
1/2 Cup mixed chopped fresh herbs,
    such as basil, oregano, thyme and parsley
1 1/2 pounds bow tie pasta,
    cooked according to package directions
Fresh herbs for garnish

Sprinkle chicken with salt and pepper. In a skillet large enough to hold chicken in a single, uncrowded layer (or you can sauté in batches) heat 1 tablespoon olive oil until very hot. Add chicken breasts, and sauté until lightly brown and just barely cooked through. Remove chicken from pan, and cut into 1/2-inch cubes. Reserve, taking care not to lose the juices.

Reheat the same skillet, and add remaining olive oil, tomatoes and mushrooms. Cook for 2 minutes. Add vinegar, then stock. Scrape bottom of pan to loosen brown bits. Add chicken with its juices. Cook over high heat until liquid is reduced by half. Add garlic, herbs, cooked pasta, salt and pepper. Toss to mix well. Garnish with sprig of fresh herbs.

Grilled Pork with Port-Infused Onions

1/4 Cup pure olive oil
3 Cups julienned onion
1 Cup port
18 slices pork tenderloin, each 1/2-inch thick
Salt and freshly ground black pepper

Heat a sauté pan over high heat for 1 minute. Add olive oil, then onions. Reduce heat to medium-low, and sauté until lightly caramelized, approximately 15 minutes. Add port, and scrape brown bits from bottom of pan. Raise heat to medium-high, and cook until liquid is reduced by half.

Season pork slices with salt and pepper. Grill or sauté quickly over high heat, approximately 2 minutes per side. Serve pork slices fanned on each plate, topped with port-infused onions.

Chocolate Pate

1/2 Cup light corn syrup
1/2 Cup butter
1 1/4 pounds semisweet chocolate,
    coarsely chopped
3 egg yolks
2 Cups heavy cream, divided
1/4 Cup powdered (10X) sugar
1 teaspoon vanilla extract

Line a loaf pan with enough plastic wrap so that the edges of wrap stick up on all four sides. Set aside.

In a 3-quart pot over medium heat melt corn syrup and butter. Add chocolate pieces, and stir constantly until melted. Blend egg yolks and 1/2 cup cream, and add to chocolate mixture. Simmer approximately 5 minutes. Do not boil. Remove from heat, and refrigerate until cooled, stirring occasionally to accelerate cooling process.

While chocolate is cooling whip remaining cream, powdered sugar and vanilla until stiff. Fold whipped cream into cooled chocolate, and pour into prepared loaf pan. Fold edges of plastic wrap over top of terrine, and refrigerate 6 to 8 hours.

Turn pate out onto a cutting board, unwrap, and slice with a hot knife. Serve with raspberry or vanilla sauce, and garnish with fresh berries or edible flowers.

Editor's Note
• *Smoked shrimp are available at Wellspring Grocery and other area gourmet stores.*

Grilled Spring Vegetables with Fresh Mozzarella and Balsamic Syrup

The Washington Duke Inn & Golf Club's Fairview Restaurant

Left to right

JOEY ABITABILO
EXECUTIVE CHEF,

MARK RHODES
CHEF,

AND

THOMAS BARRY
CHEF

The Washington Duke Inn in Durham is the recipient of 3 AAA Four Diamond Awards. The cuisine presented under the expertise of executive chef Joey Abitabilo reflects global flair. Abitabilo's specials are often a reflection of his Italian heritage coupled with his gift for depth and balance.

Moroccan Style Eggplant Soup

5 large eggplants
2/3 Cup olive oil, divided
2 Tablespoons ground cumin, divided
2 Tablespoons ground coriander, divided
1 Tablespoon ground cardamom, divided
2 1/2 Cups diced yellow onion
20 cloves garlic, sliced thin
2 Cups chopped fresh tomatoes
4 Cups peeled and chopped russet potatoes
2 quarts chicken stock
2/3 Cup chopped fresh parsley
1/3 Cup chopped fresh cilantro
2 teaspoons cayenne pepper

Remove stems from eggplant, cut each in half vertically, and score deeply in diagonal grid patter. Be careful not to puncture skin. Toss eggplants with olive oil, reserving 1 tablespoon oil for later use. Sprinkle with 1 tablespoon cumin, 1 tablespoon coriander and 1 1/2 teaspoons cardamom, and roast eggplants flesh side down on baking sheet in 350°F oven. Remove eggplants from oven when very soft. Cool, and scoop out pulp, discarding skin. Set aside.

Sauté onions in remaining tablespoon olive oil over medium heat until lightly browned. Add garlic, and sauté until garlic is soft. Add remaining cumin, coriander and cardamom, stirring briskly. Add potatoes and stock. Bring to a boil, and immediately lower to simmer. Add tomatoes, cayenne pepper and eggplant pulp. Simmer 15 minutes or until everything is very soft. Season to taste.

Puree soup in blender, and strain puree through a coarse-mesh strainer. Add chopped parsley and cilantro, taste and adjust seasoning if necessary.

Grilled Spring Vegetables with Fresh Mozzarella and Balsamic Syrup

24 large asparagus spears
3 red bell peppers
3 Tablespoons olive oil, divided
4 Cups balsamic vinegar
3 Tablespoons fresh thyme
Salt and freshly ground black pepper
2 red onions, peeled and sliced into
    1/8-inch slices
3 yellow squash, sliced into 1/8-inch slices
1 1/2 pounds fresh mozzarella cheese, sliced

Snap off, and discard woody bottoms from asparagus. Plunge asparagus spears into boiling water for 1 minute. Remove, and immediately plunge into ice water. Remove asparagus from water, pat dry, and set aside.

Rub bell peppers with 2 teaspoons olive oil, and roast in a 450°F oven until blistered all over. (Or, using tongs hold each pepper over gas flame until skin is blackened.) When peppers are blistered drop them into a paper bag, and close bag tightly. Remove peppers from bag after 5 minutes, and peel and discard skin. Cut peppers open, remove and discard seeds. Cut each pepper into 1/2-inch strips. Reserve.

Preheat charcoal grill to medium-high heat. Toss all vegetables in remaining olive oil, thyme, salt and pepper. Place onions on grill first, and cook for 2 minutes. Add squash, and cook for 1 minute. Add asparagus and red peppers, and cook only until grill marks are pronounced. Remove all vegetables from grill, and reserve.

For the Balsamic syrup
Pour balsamic vinegar into small saucepan over medium-low heat. Simmer until liquid is reduced by two thirds. Reduce heat to low, and watch carefully as it continue to reduce. The bubbles will become larger, and you will see the liquid begin to thicken. Be careful not to let the vinegar burn. When thickened remove balsamic syrup from heat, and allow syrup to cool in the saucepan.

To assemble
Place 1 mozzarella slice in center of each of 6 oven-proof plates. Put plates in a 300°F oven for 2 minutes. Remove plates, and pile grilled vegetables on top of cheese. Drizzle with balsamic syrup, and serve.

Capellini with Shiitake Mushrooms and Goat Cheese

1 1/2 pounds DeCecco® Capellini pasta
5 Tablespoons light olive oil, divided
1 pound shiitake mushrooms, stemmed
    and sliced
1 pound fresh spinach, cleaned and stemmed
1 Tablespoon minced garlic
1 Cup white wine
2 Cups chicken stock
3/4 Cup extra virgin olive oil
4 ounces Montrechet-type goat cheese
Salt and freshly ground black pepper

Blanch capellini in salted boiling water for 4 minutes or until al dente. Drain pasta and plunge into ice water. Drain pasta again, and toss with 1 tablespoon olive oil. Set aside.

In a sauté pan over medium-high heat add light olive oil. When hot add mushrooms, and sauté until golden. Add garlic, and stir for 30 seconds. Add white wine, and reduce liquid by half. Add chicken stock, and season liberally with salt and pepper.

Add capellini, and cook over medium heat for 4 minutes. Add spinach, and mix into hot pasta until spinach wilts. There should be a little broth around the edges of the pan. If there is not enough, add more chicken stock. If there is too much broth, and it looks soupy, pour of excess liquid. Remove pasta from heat, and add extra virgin olive oil. Stir to incorporate. Serve in pasta bowls with goat cheese crumbled over top.

Roast Chicken Risotto with Saffron, Grilled Corn and Tomatoes

1 chicken (4-pounds)
1 lemon, cut in half
5 garlic cloves
3 sprigs fresh rosemary
3 ears fresh corn
Salt and freshly ground black pepper
1 3/4 Cups diced yellow onion
3 Tablespoons olive oil
2 Cups Arborio rice
5 strands saffron
Pinch crushed red pepper flakes
1 Cup white wine
1 1/2 Cups diced tomatoes
1 quart chicken stock
3 Cups loosely packed fresh spinach leaves
1/2 Cup julienned basil leaves
1/2 Cup aged Parmigiano-Reggiano cheese
3 Tablespoons butter

To Roast the Chicken

Rinse chicken inside and out with cold water. Stuff with lemon halves, garlic cloves and rosemary sprigs. Roast in a 375°F oven until juice runs clear when pricked at the thigh joint, approximately 40 minutes. Cool. Remove and discard skin. Pick the meat from the carcass avoiding any gristle, fat or bones. Reserve meat.

For the Corn

Husk corn, and rub with olive oil, salt and pepper. Grill over medium-hot coals until speckled with light char marks. Cool, and remove kernels from cob. Reserve kernels.

For the Risotto

In a large heavy-bottom saucepan over medium heat, sauté onions in 3 tablespoons olive oil for 5 minutes. Do not brown. When onions are translucent add rice, and stir with wooden spoon to coat rice with oil. Add saffron and red pepper flakes. Stir constantly. Add white wine and tomatoes, and stir until liquid is absorbed. Add chicken stock 1 ladle at a time, stirring until each ladleful is incorporated before adding the next.

When rice is almost tender, after about 20 minutes, add corn and chicken, and cook for 5 more minutes. Adjust seasoning with salt and pepper. Risotto is done when there is just a little bite at the center of each grain of rice. When tender add spinach, basil, cheese and butter. Stir until spinach wilts. Serve immediately.

Macerated Berries with Orange Marsala Zabaglione

1 1/2 pints ripe strawberries
1 1/2 pints ripe raspberries or blackberries
2 Tablespoons balsamic vinegar
2 Tablespoons sugar

Carefully clean berries discarding any twigs and stems. Cut strawberries in halves or quarters, and place in a glass bowl. Add raspberries, then add vinegar and sugar, and toss gently. Set aside to macerate.

For the Zabaglione

8 egg yolks
1 Cup Marsala wine
4 Tablespoons sugar
1 Cup orange juice
3 teaspoons lemon zest

Use a stainless steel bowl that will fit over (not in) a pot of boiling water. Add egg yolks to bowl, and whisk to combine. Add remaining ingredients, and whisk to combine. Place bowl over pot of boiling water, and whisk constantly. Yolks should get frothy, then form a custard. When custard looks thick, drag a wooden spoon across bottom of bowl. Spoon should leave a stripe. Taste for sweetness, adjust and chill.

To Assemble

Whisk chilled zabaglione custard lightly to make it fluid. If it is too thick, thin with a little cream or milk. Place a spoonful or 2 into an attractive glass. Add a few berries, then more sauce, then more berries, ending with zabaglione.

North Carolina Blue Crab and Corn Bisque

Sautéed Red Snapper with Black-Eyed Pea Cake

The Weathervane
at A Southern Season

**DEVON MILLS
EXECUTIVE CHEF**

The Weathervane at A Southern Season in Chapel Hill is a comfortable cafe set in the midst of one of the Triangle's busiest, and most lavish, gourmet specialty stores. Executive chef Devon Mills ably presents a menu with dishes that range from simple to exotic. The garden is a popular spot for al fresco dining. And, don't forget the myriad international specialties and housewares in the store.

▼▼▼▼▼▼▼▼▼▼▼▼▼▼▼▼▼▼▼▼▼▼▼▼▼▼▼▼▼▼▼

North Carolina Blue Crab and Corn Bisque

1 Cup diced applewood smoked bacon
5 Tablespoons all-purpose flour
1 Cup minced onion
1/2 Cup sliced shallots
1 Cup fresh corn kernels
2 fresh corn cobs, kernels removed
1/4 teaspoon ground white pepper
3 bay leaves
1 teaspoon dried tarragon
1/2 teaspoon saffron threads
1 Cup white wine
1 Cup clam juice
4 1/2 Cups chicken stock
1 1/2 Cups heavy cream
2 teaspoons salt
2 Tablespoons lemon juice
1 pound fresh lump crabmeat
1/3 Cup snipped chives

In a small sauté pan over low heat slowly cook bacon until crispy. Drain bacon, reserve fat, and set both aside. [See *Editor's Note*]

Using the same sauté pan, place 1/4 cup reserved bacon fat in pan, and whisk in flour to make a roux. Cook over medium heat until roux turns a light nutmeg brown. Set aside.

Add 2 tablespoons bacon fat to a 4-quart saucepan over medium heat. Add onions, shallots, corn kernels, and corn cobs which have each been cut into 3 pieces. Gently cook until vegetables are soft, but not colored. Add white pepper, bay leaves, saffron and tarragon, and mix thoroughly.

Add white wine, and reduce liquid by half. Add clam juice and chicken stock. Bring to a boil. Transfer 1 cup liquid to pan where with reserved roux, whisking to completely combine. Pour roux back into soup, bring to a boil, reduce heat, and gently simmer for 20 minutes.

Remove and discard corn cobs, and add heavy cream. Continue simmering for 5 minutes. Remove pan from heat. Remove bay leaves from pan, and place mixture in food processor or blender. Puree. Push puree through a medium-mesh strainer to remove solids. Add salt and lemon juice, and stir to combine. Place a portion of lump crabmeat in each of 6 large soup bowls, and pour soup on top. Garnish with crumbled smoked bacon and chives.

Potato Pancake with Lettuces, Parmesan and Pine nuts

6 Cups peeled, grated Idaho potatoes
  [See *Editor's Note*]
2 Tablespoons finely minced garlic
1/4 Cup chopped fresh thyme
  (1 teaspoon dried)
Salt and freshly ground black pepper
Pure olive oil for frying
1 pound mesclun or mixed lettuces
1/4 Cup lemon juice
1/4 Cup olive oil
1/2 Cup pine nuts, toasted
1/4 pound shaved Parmesan cheese

Mix grated potatoes, garlic, thyme, salt and pepper, and divide into 6 equal portions. Coat a 6-inch non-stick skillet with olive oil. Place skillet over medium heat. When hot add single portion of potato mixture in middle. Use a metal spatula to flatten potato mixture to 1/2-inch thick, and shape into a circle. Sauté for 5 or 6 minutes until golden brown. Turn cake over, and cook other side until crispy. Place pancake on paper towels to drain. Mix olive oil and lemon juice. Toss with mesclun. To serve, place each potato pancake on a plate, top with tightly mounded greens. Garnish with toasted pinenuts and shaved Parmesan.

Fried Oysters with Mushrooms, Greens and Pearl Onions

For the Pearl Onions
  1 pint pearl onions, skins removed
Poach onions in boiling, salted water for 7 to 10 minutes or until tender. Drain, and set aside.

For the Mushroom Vinaigrette
  6 Tablespoons pure olive oil
  1/2 pound crimini mushrooms, quartered
  1 pound shiitake mushrooms, quartered
  2 1/2 Tablespoons minced garlic
  2 Tablespoons minced shallots
  1 Cup minced red bell pepper
  1/2 Cup minced red onion
  1/4 Cup balsamic vinegar
  3 Tablespoons extra virgin olive oil
  1 1/2 Tablespoons lemon juice
  1 Tablespoon lemon zest
  2 teaspoons salt
  2 teaspoons freshly ground black pepper

  3 Tablespoons chopped fresh oregano
    (1/2 teaspoon dried)
  1/2 pound fresh spinach, cleaned and cut into
    chiffonade [See *Cook's Notes & Glossary*]
In large skillet heat pure olive oil until it begins to smoke. Add all mushrooms, and sauté until they start to turn crispy. Turn off heat, and add garlic, shallots, onions and bell peppers. Stir to combine. Add balsamic vinegar, extra virgin olive oil, lemon juice, lemon zest, salt, pepper and oregano. Turn heat to low, and add spinach. Cook only until spinach wilts. Divide, and arrange mixture on 6 warm plates.

For the Fried Oysters
  1/2 cup all-purpose flour
  1 Cup cornmeal
  Salt and freshly ground black pepper
  1/2 teaspoon dried oregano
  30 large select oysters
  1 quart vegetable oil for frying
Blend flour, cornmeal, salt, pepper and oregano in large mixing bowl. Drain oysters, and completely coat each oyster in seasoned flour mixture.

  Heat oil to 375°F. Shake excess coating from oysters, and fry in small batches until lightly browned. Drain, then arrange 5 oysters atop each portion of mushroom vinaigrette. Serve immediately.

Sautéed Red Snapper with Black-Eyed Pea Cake

For the Black-Eyed Pea Cake
  2 Tablespoons peanut or pure olive oil
  1 Cup finely diced onion
  3/4 Cup finely diced celery
  3/4 Cup diced red bell pepper
  1 1/2 Tablespoons minced garlic
  1 small ham hock
  1 pound fresh or frozen black-eyed peas
  3 Cups chicken stock
  1/2 teaspoon dried thyme
  2 bay leaves
  1 teaspoon salt
  1 teaspoon freshly ground black pepper
  2 Tablespoons lemon juice
  1 teaspoon lemon zest
  1 egg, beaten
  2 1/4 Cups breadcrumbs
  Pure olive oil or peanut oil for frying
To a small saucepan over medium heat add 2 tablespoons oil, onions, celery, bell pepper and garlic, and sauté 5 minutes or until tender, stirring frequently. Add ham hock, black-eyed peas, chicken stock, thyme and bay leaves. Bring to a boil, reduce heat and sim-

mer for 45 minutes until peas are tender and almost all liquid has evaporated. Cool and reserve.

In a food processor or blender puree half the pea mixture, pour puree back into pot with remaining peas. Add salt, pepper, lemon juice, lemon zest, beaten egg and 1 cup breadcrumbs. Continue to add breadcrumbs until mixture is stiff. Divide mixture, and form into 6 1-inch-thick patties.

Coat bottom of non-stick skillet with oil. Sauté patties over medium-high heat until crispy on both sides. Drain on paper towels. Patties may be kept on a rack in a 200°F oven for up to 20 minutes before serving.

For the Asparagus Sauce
    5 large very ripe tomatoes
    2 teaspoons kosher salt
    1/2 teaspoon minced garlic
    1 Tablespoon minced shallots
    1/3 Cup extra virgin olive oil
    3 Tablespoons chopped fresh basil
    12 asparagus stalks cut into 2-inch lengths
Blanch asparagus in boiling water for 30 seconds, then place in ice water to cool.

Remove stem end of tomatoes, and squeeze out excess juice. Hand chop tomatoes to a pulp-like consistency (do not use a food processor). You should have approximately 3 1/2 cups tomato pulp. Place tomatoes in a bowl. Add salt, garlic and shallots, and let sit for 20 minutes until tomatoes render their liquid. Drain, and discard liquid. Add remaining ingredients, and reserve.

For the Fish
    6 snapper fillets, slashed diagonally, skin on
    Pure olive oil for frying
    Salt and freshly ground black pepper
Heat a large non-stick skillet over medium heat. Add enough olive oil to cover bottom of pan, and heat until oil begins to smoke. Carefully place fillets flesh side down in pan. Cook 1 to 3 minutes without moving fish. Then lightly shake pan; if fillets move, turn fish over, and cook 1 to 3 minutes on skin side. Sprinkle salt and pepper on top of each fillet.

Portion sauce among 6 warm plates, making sure to cover inside ring of each plate. Place warm pea cake in center of sauce, and top with snapper fillet. Serve immediately.

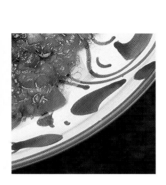

▼▼▼▼▼▼▼▼▼▼▼▼▼▼▼▼▼▼▼▼▼▼▼▼▼▼▼▼▼

Apple Walnut Tart

For the Pie Crust
    1/4 Cup chilled shortening
    1/4 Cup chilled butter
    1 1/2 Cups all-purpose flour
    1/2 teaspoon salt
    3 to 4 Tablespoons ice water
In processor with a steel blade cut shortening and butter into flour by pulsing on and off. Mixture should resemble coarse meal. Gradually add ice water, pulsing on and off until dough forms a smooth ball. Wrap in plastic wrap, and refrigerate for 30 minutes.

Spray a 10-inch tart pan with non-stick spray shortening. Roll out dough, and fit into tart pan, crimping edges to create an attractive rim.

For the Filling
    4 Tablespoons applejack or Calvados
        (apple brandy), divided
    2/3 Cup raisins
    1/2 Cup sugar
    1 Tablespoon cinnamon
    1/4 teaspoon nutmeg
    1/8 teaspoon ground cloves
    3/4 Cup coarsely chopped walnuts
    2 pounds peeled, cored and sliced apples
    4 Tablespoons melted butter
    1/2 Cup apricot preserves
    Whipped cream or crème fraîche
        for garnish (optional)
In a small non-stick skillet heat raisins in 2 tablespoons apple brandy. Bring to a boil, and turn off heat. Set aside until raisins have absorbed the liquor. In a mixing bowl blend sugar, cinnamon, nutmeg and cloves. Toss apple slices in this mixture until coated. Remove apples, and save any excess spice blend.

Toss spiced apples, walnuts and raisins together. Place in tart shell mounding apples in center, and pour melted butter evenly over top. Sprinkle with any remaining spice blend.

Bake at 450°F for 10 minutes. Reduce heat to 375°F, and bake for an additional 45 minutes or until apples are tender and have settled into tart shell. Remove from oven, and cool on cake rack.

Mix apricot preserves and 2 tablespoons apple brandy in small bowl suitable for microwave. Heat mixture on high in microwave for 45 seconds or until preserves melt. Remove from microwave, and brush over top of tart. Serve tart warm with whipped cream or crème fraîche.

Editor's Note
• *Grated Potatoes. Do not rinse the grated potatoes or they will not stick together. Potatoes will turn brown if left in the air, so grate them just before making this dish—the slight brown color will disappear when cooked.*

Avgolemono A Greek lemon and chicken soup.

Blackened Seasoning A blend of hot peppers, garlic, and other spices. Blackened Seasoning is available in powdered form in the spice section of most grocery stores.

Butter All recipes in this book calling for butter refer to sweet, unsalted butter. Unsalted butter has less water content and a higher fat content than salted butter. To keep unsalted butter fresh, store it in your freezer.

Calamari Squid Many professional chefs prefer calamari that has been frozen. They believe that freezing tenderizes the meat. In order for it to be tender, you must either cook calamari a very long time or for a very few minutes.

Chicken Stock If you clean your own house you can make chicken stock. Simply put the stock on to simmer while you vacuum and do laundry. If, however, you prefer to buy prepared chicken stock we use Health Valley® brand fat-free, unsalted chicken broth in our test kitchen.

Chiffonade Chiffonade comes from the French language and literally means "made of rags." In cooking terms it refers to shreds or thin strips of herbs or leafy greens. To make a chiffonade remove leaves from stems. Roll leaves tightly along their vertical spines, and using a very sharp knife cut them into 1/6-inch strips horizontally across the leaf. The resulting strips are called chiffonade.

Chocolate The quality of chocolate is determined by the amount of cocoa butter. Choose chocolate that is marked "Premium" or "Couverture" when making a ganache or chocolate icing.

Chop To cut food into bite-size, or smaller, pieces. Food processors can also be used to chop.

Dice To cut into 1/4-inch to 1/2-inch cubes.

Dill Butter Combine 6 tablespoons softened butter with 1 tablespoon fresh or 1 teaspoon dried dill weed.

Eggs All recipes in this book refer to large eggs. If large eggs are not available you can substitute the following for every 5 large eggs: 4 extra-large eggs, 6 medium-size eggs or 7 small eggs.

Food Mill A mechanical sieve with a hand-turned blade that forces food through a sieve or strainer.

Ganache A rich chocolate icing made by combining semisweet chocolate and heavy cream, and heating it until the chocolate melts. Ganache is usually used to glaze cakes and pastries.

Garlic, Roasted To roast your own garlic slice the stem end off a whole bulb of garlic to expose the ends of the cloves. Pour 1 teaspoon of olive oil over the cut end, then wrap the entire bulb tightly in aluminum foil and bake in a 350°F oven for 30 to 45 minutes, until the cloves have turned a nut-brown and become very soft. Roasted garlic will keep, refrigerated, for up to 3 weeks.

Garlic Butter Combine 6 tablespoons softened butter with 1 teaspoon minced fresh garlic.

Hollandaise Sauce Place 6 egg yolks in a glass bowl over, not in, boiling water. Whisk to combine. Add 5 tablespoons hot water, and whisk vigorously until bubbles form on top of mixture. Add 5 tablespoons lemon juice and continuing whisking constantly until mixture begins to thicken. When mixture is thick, remove from heat and slowly dribble 1 cup melted, salted butter into mixture while whisking constantly. When butter is completely incorporated cover bowl and place back over hot water off the heat. It will stay warm for about 1 hour.

Italian Parsley Flat leafed parsley that has a stronger and longer-lasting taste than curly parsley when cooked.

Jerk Seasoning (also called *Jamaican Jerk Seasoning*) Combine a 3-inch square piece of dried chili pepper, 1/4 teaspoon ginger, 1/4 teaspoon thyme, 1/4 inch canella stick, 1 allspice berry and 1 clove garlic in a small food processor or spice grinder. Process until pulverized.

Julienne To cut foods into thin matchstick strips, approximately 1/8-inch square and 2 1/2 inches long.

Mascarpone Cheese A slightly sweet, rich, double- or triple-cream cheese made from cow's milk, mascarpone hails from Italy and is often used to make cheesecake.

Mesclun A Provençal word for mixed baby lettuces.

Mince To cut food into very small pieces, 1/8-inch cubes or smaller.

Non-reactive Acidic and salty foods react with aluminum, copper and some other metals. When cooking with wine, citrus, tomatoes or other acidic foods use stainless steel, glass or tin-lined cookware.

Oil For Frying Use a pure vegetable oil for frying, such as peanut oil. Extra virgin olive oil burns at a very low temperature and should not be used for high-heat cooking. If a recipe calls for olive oil for cooking, use a "pure" olive oil.

Phyllo (also spelled *filo*) A paper-thin Greek pastry similar to strudel dough. Frozen phyllo is readily available in the frozen dessert section of your grocery store. The most important thing to remember is that this pastry is delicate, and tends to dry out quickly if not handled properly. Defrost the dough overnight in your refrigerator. Trying to defrost it in a microwave doesn't work, and leaving it at room temperature for several hours tends to make the leaves stick together. When you unfold the sheets and put them on the counter to begin a recipe, immediately cover the entire stack of pastry first with plastic wrap, then with a slightly damp dish towel. Use only one sheet at a time when making the recipe, and keep the rest covered.

Risotto Italian rice dish made with Arborio rice. The grains of Arborio rice are shorter and fatter than any other short-grain rice and contain more starch. It is the starch that gives risotto its creamy texture.

Roma Tomatoes Plum or Italian tomatoes.

Roux A blend of equal parts fat and flour. To make 1/3 cup of roux melt 3 tablespoons butter in a sauté pan over medium-high heat, and add 3 tablespoons of flour. Stir constantly with a whisk until golden. Take off heat, and reserve. Before adding a roux to a boiling liquid temper it by adding about 1 cup of hot liquid to the roux and whisking to combine the 2 liquids. Then, pour the tempered liquid back into the pot of boiling liquid.

Sauté To cook food quickly in a skillet or sauté pan over direct heat using a small amount of fat.

Tahini A thick paste made from ground sesame seeds, it is usually found in Middle Eastern recipes. Tahini is available in most grocery stores. Hannaford's stocks tahini in their "International" section.

Water Bath Also called a *bain marie*, a water bath is usually used to cook delicate foods such as custards. To make a water bath place the dish containing the food to be cooked in a larger pan. Pour boiling water into the larger pan to come half way

careful not to splash water into the dish containing the food. Place the entire water bath in a preheated oven and cook as directed.

Zest The outer skin of a citrus fruit. Make sure that you do not retain any of the white pith just below the skin. It will impart a very bitter flavor.

Substitutions

Even though you should assemble all of the ingredients listed for a recipe before you begin to cook—so that you will know what is missing before you arrive at a critical stage without a critical ingredient—there are times when you will find yourself without an ingredient needed to complete a recipe. Following are some possible substitutions.

Baking Powder, 1 teaspoon

Substitute 1/4 teaspoon baking soda, plus 5/8 teaspoon cream of tartar.

Buttermilk, 1 Cup

Substitute 1 Cup plain yogurt, or 1 Tablespoon vinegar or lemon juice plus enough milk to equal 1 Cup liquid. Allow to rest for 5 minutes.

Cornstarch, 1 Tablespoon

Substitute 2 Tablespoons all-purpose flour, or 2 teaspoons arrowroot.

Sour Cream, 1 Cup

Substitute 1 Tablespoon lemon juice plus evaporated whole milk to equal 1 Cup.

Tomato Sauce

Substitute 3/8 Cup tomato paste plus 1/2 Cup water.

Common Measurement Equivalents

3 teaspoons = 1 Tablespoon

1/2 Tablespoon = 1 1/2 teaspoons

2 Tablespoons = 1 fluid ounce

4 Tablespoons = 1/4 Cup

1 stick butter = 8 Tablespoons butter

Baking Pan Volume

8″ x 8″ x 1/2″ = 6 Cups

8″ x 8″ x 2″ = 8 Cups

9″ x 9″ x 1 1/2″ = 8 Cups

9″ x 9″ x 2″ = 10 Cups

13″ x 9″ x 2″ = 15 Cups

8″ x 4″ x 2 1/2″ loaf = 4 Cups

8″ x 1 1/2″ round cake = 4 Cups

9″ x 1 1/2″ round cake = 6 Cups

10″ x 2″ round cake = 10 3/4 Cups

9 1/2″ x 2 1/2″ springform = 10 Cups

10″ x 2 1/2″ springform = 12 Cups

Cards

To order additional copies of

American Express® Presents Top Chefs of the Triangle

Call or write:

Raleigh Magazine

5 West Hargett Street

Suite 809

Raleigh, NC 27601

Phone 919. 755. 9200

Fax 919. 755. 9201

Toll Free 1. 800. 252. 8476

You may order On-Line at RaleighMag@Raleigh.VCN.com

Additional copies may be ordered for $28.50 per copy plus $5 for postage, and handling. North Carolina residents add 6% sales tax ($1.71). Make checks payable to *Raleigh Magazine.* Include your complete mailing address. You may charge your order with your American Express Card. Please include the card's expiration date, exact name as it appears on your card and mailing address.

A portion of all proceeds from the sale of *American Express® Presents Top Chefs of The Triangle* will be donated to The Inter-Faith Food Shuttle, which rescues thousands of pounds of prepared and perishable food each day and immediately transports it to soup kitchens and shelters feeding the Triangle's poor and homeless people. In 1995, more than 100 volunteers collected in excess of 2,000,000 pounds of food which created almost 1,500,000 meals—all at no charge—all without taxpayer funds.

A portion of the proceeds will also be donated to Share Our Strength's Taste of the Nation. Presented by American Express and Calphalon, Taste of the Nation is the largest nationwide culinary benefit to fight hunger. An annual series of food and wine tastings are held in April in more than 100 cities across the country. Since 1988, Taste of the Nation events have raised more than $22,000,000. One hundred percent of ticket sales are distributed to anti-hunger organizations.